Reclaim the Power
of the Witch

Reclaim the Power of the Witch

Making Magic Make Sense

Monte Plaisance

WEISERBOOKS
Boston, MA/York Beach, ME

First published in 2001 by
Red Wheel/Weiser, LLC
P. O. Box 612
York Beach, ME 03910-0612
www.redwheelweiser.com

Note to the reader: This book is intended as an informational guide. The remedies, approaches, and techniques described herein are meant to supplement, and not to be a substitute for, professional medical care or treatment. They should not be used to treat a serious ailment without prior consultation with a qualified healthcare professional.

Library of Congress Cataloging-in-Publication Data

Plaisance, Monte.
    Reclaim the power of the witch/Monte Plaisance.
        p. cm.
    ISBN 1-57863-195-5 (pbk.: alk. paper)
        1. Witchcraft. I. Title.

BF1566.P53 2001
133.4'3—dc21   2001026123

Typeset in Adobe Garamond

Printed in Canada

TCP

08 07 06 05 04 03 02 01
8 7 6 5 4 3 2 1

The paper used in this publication meets the minimum requirements of the American National Standard for Information Sciences-Permanence of Paper for Printed Library Materials Z39.48-1992 (R1997).

Contents

Contents

Thessalonian Witch's Prayer

O' Night, most faithful to these my Mysteries, and ye golden Stars, who with the Moon, succeed the fires of the day, and thou, three-faced Hekate, who comest conscious of my design, and ye charms and acts of the enchanters, and thou, too, Earth that does furnish the enchanters with powerful herbs; ye breezes, too, and winds, mountains, rivers and lakes, and all ye Deities of the groves, and all ye Gods of night attend here; through whose aid, whenever I will, the rivers run back from their astonished banks to their sources, and by my charms I calm the troubled sea, and rouse it when calm; I dispense the clouds and I bring clouds upon the Earth; I both allay the winds and I raise them; and I break the jaws of serpents with my words and my spells; I move too, the solid rocks, and the oaks torn up with their own native earth, and the forests as well; I command the mountains, too, to quake, and the Earth to groan, and the ghosts to come forth from their tombs. Thee, too, O Moon, do I draw down, although the Temesaean Brass relieves thy pangs. By my spells, also, the chariot of my grandaire is rendered pale; Aurora, too, is pale through my enchantments.

Introduction

It was a common practice among ancient authors to begin their literary works with a hymn or prayer to the gods, to bless the words that followed. I try, to the best of my ability, to follow the ancient ways, so I think it right to begin this work with a short devotion to the gods, and then to inform my reader, in a few words, who and what I am, in what circumstances I am placed, and why I undertook the task of writing this book.

O Ancient Gods and Goddesses of Old,
Sing to me of days gone by, that I may learn Your ways,
And let me render to those who read these words
Those songs which you have given to me.

The first thing that put me on the road to witchcraft was an experience I had as a child. I was involved in an accident that caused me to have a near-death experience. When I was brought back to consciousness, I awoke with a desire to learn as much as I could about spiritual matters and the occult.

I could not find a teacher, so, just like most of you out there, I bought books and studied, practiced, and learned. Most of the books left me thirsting for more knowledge, so I bought more books, and still the thirsting did not cease. Before I knew it, I had one of the largest occult libraries in my town.

But you see, there is a catch to this story. I not only read the books, I also performed all the exercises, rituals, and spells that were contained in them—and I was frequently disappointed with the results. All it served to do was prove to me that many authors had no practical experience with the subjects about which they professed to have knowledge. This was also the first thing that pushed me to write this book. I wanted to share with others the actual experiences I have had during my years of practicing witchcraft and magick.

The second incident that pushed me to write came after I had been studying and training for many years. I had the pleasure to meet and talk with a very competent magician who, in the course of our conversation, said that he thought witchcraft lacked any real magical power, because many of the people practicing witchcraft were focusing more on acquiring degrees and titles and focusing less on magical and spiritual training. This statement offended me at first, but after some thought I had to agree.

I explained to this person that this kind of thing happens not only in witchcraft, but also in nearly every other movement that becomes popular. Whenever a coven, group, or organization becomes mainstream, it suddenly becomes the "in thing" to do, and everyone wants to be a member. People who practice witchcraft, magick, or anything else, for that matter, simply because they feel it is the "in thing" to do are usually only interested in titles or degrees. These people feel that owning a title from a particular group or organization makes them an "authority" in their field of study. Fortunately, they are easy to spot; just watch how quickly they show you those certificates and how slow they are to give you any useful information.

Titles are nice, but they do not make a person a witch. A fancy certificate on the wall of a doctor's office does not make him or her a better physician. It is the desire to heal that makes a great doctor.

Witchcraft is a religion of freedom and understanding, teaching perfect love and perfect trust, yet I have found that many do not follow these tenets. So I decided to write this book to give a practical understanding of the philosophical aspects of witchcraft and how they can be applied in life.

The third, and probably the most important, reason I finally decided to write this book is because most of the books currently available on witchcraft focus on the religious aspects of witchcraft, with only a brief glimpse of the magical practices. Also, many covens do not cover magick in depth, but only touch on the basics and leave the students to thresh out the details on their own from various sources. Most of these sources are written in a Judeo-Christian Ceremonial theme, which explains the hodgepodge of words often used in some Wiccan rites. With this book, I hope to supply you with a useful and authentic source of material to help you further your studies in the craft. In essence, I wrote this book for those of you out there who want to reclaim the power of the witch.

Every religion throughout history has had its magicians, shamans, and miracle workers, and the modern witchcraft movement has taken on many faces that revolve around these ancient religious practices, especially the religious beliefs of the ancient Celts. However, I begin the history of witchcraft with the religions of ancient Greece and Rome.

The reason for this is that Greek and Roman culture is still a fundamental part of all European culture and, by extension, all American culture as well. It is important to remember that Alexander the Great conquered most of the known world of his time, and everywhere he went, he carried Greek culture with him. When Rome conquered Greece in 146 B.C.E., the Romans were overwhelmed by the sophistication of Greek culture, and they adopted many of the Greek ways of life. The Roman Empire in turn spread to the North African coast and extended north across the English Channel. Therefore the Greco-Roman tradition has been a part of the culture of much of the world for over 2000 years. As Percy Shelley quite rightly said in the preface to his work *Hellas: A Lyrical Drama*, "We are all Greeks."

The Greek gods have also been close to the center of Western culture, and Greek mythology is still a major influence in literature, art, and language today. In fact, many witchcraft rituals are patterned on those of the ancient Greeks and Romans. Understand that what I am saying is that Greek and Roman religions are a good source for magical and religious information pertaining to the practices of witchcraft, but they are not superior to any other ancient or modern source.

Of the Greek and Roman gods, the most important to the practice of witchcraft is the goddess Hekate, the patroness of witches since the most ancient of times. Hekate is depicted as having three faces and standing at the crossroads, where She can watch all that goes by. In a sense, She is the mediator between this world and all other worlds, which gives her an important role in the practice of magick. I will explain this further in the chapters that follow.

This book is the culmination of much research and practice, and within these pages I have shared many of my experiences and some of the problems I have come across in my training and practices. Many of the stories may seem fantastical and hard to believe, but they are the truth. Remember that the life of a witch should be filled with magick and mystery. But do not take my word for it. I simply ask you to study and use the techniques that I present here and judge their effectiveness for yourself. Only then will you understand that knowledge can only lead to wisdom if that knowledge is put to practical use in your life.

In Love and Light,

Monte Plaisance (2001)

CHAPTER 1

WITCHCRAFT IN ANCIENT GREECE AND ROME

What witch, what magician will be able to free you from Thessalian sorceries?

—HORACE, ROMAN POET

It is a known historical fact that in classical times, magical processes were used by the ancient Greeks and Romans to produce a myriad of effects ranging anywhere from causing rain and stopping hailstorms to healing animals and increasing one's wealth. In addition to the beneficial uses of magical power, there was also a widespread use of magick for destructive purposes, such as destroying an enemy's crops or even causing a person to die. There was also a strong belief in erotic magical techniques (see The Great Rite, chapter 12). Thus it is important when thinking about the techniques of magick, especially the magick of the ancients, to take into account the motive behind the spell. To give a modern example, if a person shoots and kills an animal and uses it to feed a hungry family, it would be considered a positive thing in our society's eyes. However, if you shoot and kill an animal without reason, that is considered a wrongful act. In both cases the result is the death of an animal, and in both cases a gun is used, but the intention behind the use of the gun is what determines whether the act is good or bad.

Thus the practice of magick for beneficent purposes was considered necessary in Greece and Rome, and written laws existed that allowed for it. Magick was practiced by a wide variety of people ranging from priests and priestesses of specific deities to doctors and even thieves!

Divination was also of extreme importance to the Greeks and Romans, and the oracles of ancient times are a testament to this desire to know what the future holds. The governments of both Greece and Rome supported those whose business it was to foretell of future events or solve dilemmas that affected the people of the state or town.

On the other side of the coin, those who practiced magick with the intent of causing harm or destruction were scorned, and laws were made to condemn those guilty of this practice. Death was the usual sentence for those found guilty of performing or even attempting or professing to perform magick to bring destruction. These magicians who practiced maleficent magick were often reported to use certain objects and incantations to threaten the gods into doing their will. Thus they could circumvent the fates and produce a myriad of "miracles." While this method of threatening is not recommended to the reader, it is interesting to note that it was a common practice in the days of old.

With just a small amount of research into ancient history you will quickly find that the rituals used within the framework of *most* modern Wiccan groups are based on the Rites of Dionysus, Orpheus, and Eleusis in ancient Greece and Rome. Gerald Gardner mentions in his book *Witchcraft Today* that upon visiting the Villa of Mysteries in Pompeii he noticed striking similarities between the reliefs depicted there and the rites of witchcraft, particularly the initiation rite. The Villa consists of a large hall the walls of which are painted with twenty-nine nearly life-sized figures that depict what appears to be the initiation of a young female into the mysteries of Dionysus. These rites often passed the initiate through a series of "tests" in which he or she was allowed to watch a reenactment of the life of a deity. Particularly in the festivals of Dionysus and Eleusis, there was also a symbolic death and rebirth of the initiate along with the deity, thus making the connection, on a subconscious level, of the inner divinity of the initiate. It is my opinion that the modern witchcraft movement is primarily patterned on these ancient Greek and Roman rites of initiation and is not entirely Celtic in origin, as some believe. Why else would the traditional witch's goddess and god be Diana and Pan, both Greco-Roman deities?

Another indication that the origins of witchcraft were in the rites of the ancient Greeks is the famous witch's chant of "Eo Evohe." I have used this chant on many occasions, and not one person, whether a high priest or high priestess, has ever been able to answer to me what the words mean. They simply say that it is traditional and that it works, which it does. Now, I understand that the origin of something is not quite as important as the effectiveness of it, but my natural curiosity always pushes me to know why. So I delved deep into the books and found the origin of the word and what it meant. In Gardner's version of the *Book of Shadows*, he makes reference to the Greek call of *Evoe Evoe*—much like the *Eo Evoe* of modern witches. The origins of this chant began with the festival of Dionysus/Bacchus. During this festival, female priestesses of the god would consume large amounts of wine and work themselves into a frenzy. After this they would run through the fields and shout the words *Evoe, Bacche! O Iacche! Io Bacche! Evoe Sabae!* Eventually the festival no longer was practiced, and the words were only remembered in the minds of those who partook or witnessed the rites. The words eventually became altered into the witch's *Eo Evoe*. But what do the words mean? Well, they are derived from a myth associated with the god Dionysus/Bacchus. When the young god had slain a giant, Zeus complimented him by saying: *"Evie Evoe,"* which means, "Well done, son." So there you have it. When you chant the rhythmic and powerful *Eo Evoe,* you are intoning the words of Zeus himself.

Gardner was not the only person who implied that the origins of some witchcraft rituals are rooted in ancient Greece and Rome. There was also a witch who lived in England in the later half of the 1800s who was a most influential, though obscure, figure. This man was called George Pickengill. Old George was a notorious figure who was said to have been the leader of nine covens in England. It is rumored that Gerald Gardner was initiated into one of these covens. Many of these stories are mere speculations on the part of various individuals, but some do make strong points.

One of the stories of Old George was that he calculated astrologically and/or through spiritual means that the priests and priestesses of ancient Greece and Rome would begin to be reincarnated in the later half of the twentieth century. Therefore, he devised a series of rituals patterned on the ancient Greek and Roman rites so that the rituals would strike a familiar cord with these reincarnated priests and priestesses. These rituals were the beginning of modern Wicca.

Pickengill's reason for wanting to reinstate the ancient practices was so that there would be a religion that could "dethrone" Christianity. It seems to have worked, because Wicca has become one of the fastest growing religions in the world. Pickengill himself was a loyal devotee of the god Pan and one of the most adept magicians since Merlin. If the stories surrounding the man are even remotely true, then he was an incredible magical practitioner. I have attempted several times to communicate with the spirit of Old George, but with no success. Maybe in the future I will have better luck and get greater insight.

HEKATE AND THE WITCHES OF THESSALY

Perhaps no area of the ancient world generated more awe and fear than the region of Greece known as Thessaly. Thessaly is, according to the Greeks, the birthplace of witchcraft. Thessaly, also home to Mount Olympus, was known primarily for its witches. The witches of Thessaly were much sought after—and feared—in ancient times. They had the power to conjure the spirits of the world, cause storms or stop them, raise the dead, restore youth to the old, and draw the planets down from the sky. In fact, the modern witchcraft practice of Drawing Down the Moon is said to have originated with the Greek witches of Thessaly. However, the modern version of this practice is to call the goddess of the Moon down into the priestess of the coven. In ancient times, Drawing Down the Moon was a ritual designed to secure the love of another. It entailed a rather long and drawn out ritual that is still known to the witches of Thessaly today and is a closely guarded secret.

One of the greatest witches who frequented Thessaly was the famed Medea, of whom mythology records so much. Other witches of Thessaly have found their names surviving in the stories and myths of the ancients; Erictho and Canidia are just two that could be mentioned off hand. These women were human, yet possessed powers almost equal to those of goddesses. Now, I understand that these women were called sorceresses and magicians, but they were also called witches.

When we look back at the mythology associated with the witches of ancient Greece, we find that the Moon was considered to be the mother of the magical arts of witchcraft. Thus the goddess Diana, who is closely related to the Moon, became the queen of all witches. Diana, or Artemis in her Greek form, has gone through many changes in her worship. Originally she was a chaste goddess of the hunt and was followed by a band of female worshippers that men were forbidden to touch under penalty of death—not exactly conducive to a fertility religion. In later years at the town of Ephesus, she was seen as Diana the Many-Breasted and became a mother goddess. Selene, another goddess of the Moon, is mentioned in Theocritus. But if we delve just a little deeper, we find that there is another goddess associated with the Moon: Hekate, a goddess with a more obscure nature as far as mythology goes. It seems that she is only mentioned in writings when talking of witches and witchcraft. Even Shakespeare's witches of *Macbeth* petitioned this triple goddess.

Hekate is viewed as having three faces, one looking to the Underworld (land of the dead), one looking to the Middle World (Earth), and one looking to the Upper World (spiritual plane). There is some evidence to show that she played a part in the early rites of Eleusis, as she was the only one who saw Hades' abduction of Persephone and was also the only one who could guide Persephone back from the Underworld. In later years, Hermes replaced Hekate as the one who retrieved Persephone. This may actually be mythologically valid, as Hekate and Hermes were known to be lovers. Perhaps it was the two together who rescued the abducted goddess. It is because of her "triple vision" that Hekate is often called "the far-seeing one."

Hekate never assumed any rank in the hierarchy of Mount Olympus. Although considered a minor deity in comparison to the Olympic gods and goddesses, she is the most powerful of all deities in the realm of magick and mystery, her power being second only to Zeus himself, who nevertheless favored her. Her sacred places were crossroads and graveyards, and even common families would leave offerings of food to her at these sacred places in hopes of gathering favor with this most powerful goddess. These offerings were called "Hekate's suppers."

Initially, the region of Karia, which is now Asia Minor, was the center of Hekate worship, but she was also very well known and revered in Thessaly. Hekate is a mysterious deity around whom secret orders and ideas of magick can easily develop. She is often mistakenly portrayed as a haggard old crone with snakes in her hair, wandering about the graveyards, causing havoc with her magick. From a purely historical point of view, Hekate has never been depicted in statues or artwork from the ancient world as a crone. She is always a young, vibrant maiden, and anyone who works closely with her will soon find out that she is very active with her followers. Her depiction as a crone may come from the fact that, as a goddess, she is filled with wisdom and is rather harsh in the demands she places on her priests and priestesses. Wisdom is often a trait of crone goddesses.

The relationship with Hekate is a two-way street; she provides for you, but when she is in need of a favor she expects to be treated in kind. Hekate is truly a most wondrous goddess, albeit a harsh teacher and very demanding. I speak of this from experience, as Hekate is my patron goddess, and my life and ways are devoted primarily to her.

CHAPTER 2

WITCHCRAFT AND THE ART THEREOF

Medea was mistress of magic herbs and could bestow youth and invulnerability, calm storms and even "call down the moon," a famous love-charm said to have emanated from Thessaly....

—C. J. S THOMPSON, *THE MYSTERIES AND SECRETS OF MAGIC*

Before going any further into this book, I would like to state, very clearly, the difference between witchcraft and what witches often refer to as the "art" or the "craft." Witchcraft, or Wicca, is a religion based on the rhythms and cycles of nature. It is a way of life that dictates how we, as witches, can live in harmony with the world around us.

The religion of the craft is filled with spirits, fairies, gods and goddesses, holidays, festivals, and devotions. Witchcraft holds eight days within the course of a year's time to be sacred and worthy of celebration. These days coincide with the natural changes of the seasons and the times that lie midway between the seasons. These are days on which a person who is psychically sensitive can "feel" a difference in the energies. These days are magical and spiritual times that we must learn to tune into in order to have a smooth life. In and of itself, this aspect of witchcraft can stand alone as a spiritual path to enlightenment and happiness.

13

Since witchcraft has made its way back from the shadows of persecution, a huge focus on this religious aspect of the craft has arisen. Our tenets of belief, our rituals of celebration, even many of our healing and attuning techniques have been exposed and used by many people. Most of the information out today paints a very lovely—and true—picture of what witchcraft is. Witchcraft is a religion of love and beauty.

However, there is also the side of witchcraft that very few authors have discussed in detail, and that is magick. A witch is a magician of the highest order. Let no one turn that fact aside by saying, "Oh, you practice low magick or folk magick." The simple fact remains that a witch's magick in ancient times was the power sought after most by those who needed help.

Indeed, when people first come to learn about witchcraft these days, it is mostly because they feel that there is something in witchcraft that fills a void in their lives. This void is magick. Magick is truly the power that makes the world go round.

CONCERNING WITCHCRAFT AND CHRISTIANITY

By vilifying and running down the religion of the ancients, they [Christian priests] have thought they could persuade their votaries that their new religion was necessary for the good of mankind: a religion which in consequence of their corruptions, has been found to be in practice much worse and more injurious to the interests of society than the old one. For, from these corruptions the Christian religion . . . has not brought peace, but a sword!

—GODFREY HIGGANS, *ANACALYPSIS*

Magick has, for the most part, been taken out of Christian practices, save for some smaller groups of Christians who practice power raising in group prayers. So when people come to learn about witchcraft, they are fascinated by the art of witchcraft. When, however, they learn that there is a religion behind all of this magick, they become somewhat uncomfortable.

I have been asked on several occasions, "Can someone be a Christian and a witch?" This question was one that puzzled me at first. There are many similarities between Christianity and witchcraft, especially in the Catholic faith. Could someone choose Christ and Mary as their patron deities? I supposed it was possible, so for some time my answer was, "I suppose it could be possible." After further years of practice and having looked at other traditions of witchcraft, I have changed this point of view, and let me explain why.

I can remember my first time praying to a pagan god when I first came to witchcraft. I knew nothing of the craft at all but had devised a prayer to the Norse god Odin because at that time I was studying rune divination and sought for more knowledge. So, in my usual fashion, I went straight to the source. I performed my short prayer and ran from the room in utter fear of what I had just done. Would I go to hell for this? Would I be struck down by an angry god? I tossed and turned in my sleep that night, and finally my dreams came to me.

I saw the god Odin sitting upon a large stone throne, and on his shoulders sat a raven with golden eyes. The raven stood out to me more than anything else, and it still remains my spiritual animal. However, Odin looked at me with his one eye, the other patched over, and smiled. In a voice that was indescribably authoritative, he told me that my path was not with him and to look elsewhere for the answers I wanted. I awoke with a jerk and realized immediately that I had just heard the voice of a god!

How was it, I wondered, that whenever I prayed to the Christian god, I received no such answers through dreams or any other means? At that stage in my life, I was very stubborn, and some would say that has not changed, but I did not heed Odin's advice and continued to study and work with the Norse pantheon. Later on, I was forced to stop working with them for reasons that only a small handful of people who were camping in the woods with me at the time know about. Safe to say, it was a shattering experience for everyone that witnessed it. Regardless of all that, I continued in my search for spiritual wisdom and enlightenment, and paganism was the path that I had chosen.

Where is this story going? Well, what I want to say is that if you are going to practice witchcraft, do it with every fiber of your being. Do it with every ounce of your heart and do not hold fast to the religion to which you once belonged. If you feel the need to go to another source for spiritual wisdom, then your current path, be it Christian or whatever, is obviously not fulfilling your needs. Therefore it lacks something that you desperately wish to have. If you only put your foot in the water, you will never learn to swim. But if you jump with both feet, you do not have a choice.

I know this sounds somewhat cruel, but the way of a witch is not for the faint of heart, nor is it a path for cowards. Be brave and strong and proud of the history that you are carrying behind you. Many people have willingly given their lives in order to safeguard the secrets that are so freely taken for granted in this day and age. Do not lose the mystery of witchcraft and do not taint it by making it something that it was never meant to be. Understand that I do not condemn those who follow the Christian faith, I am simply stating that Christianity has never filled my life with the magick that witchcraft has. For others, Christianity may do so.

CONCERNING THE PRACTICING OF MAGICK

Not all witches today practice magick for the public. Very few witches that I know will open their abilities to the public out of fear of persecution or perhaps fear of ridicule or failure. As witches, we should see ourselves as the caretakers of the earth. When we come across a wounded animal, we never stop to think about the karmic repercussions of helping it (see Concerning Reincarnation and Karma, chapter 3). We simply take the animal and nurse it to health if we can. So why is it that so many witches feel that if they come across people who are in dire trouble, that magick should not be used to help nurse them back to health? Many modern practitioners will simply give people a series of spiritual exercises to perform and send them on their way. But if the person were spiritually capable of performing these exercises, he or she would not be coming to you for assistance.

When people go to a witch for magical assistance, it is because they have nowhere else to turn. Their lives are out of balance, and they need someone to show them how to get back on track. This is a great honor for the witch. These people view us with eyes of either respect or fear, because they believe that we alone can help solve their problems. Notice I say, *help* solve their problems. We cannot just solve problems, but we can help bring people back into balance, thus paving the way for them to solve the problem on their own. To do this, we must find the source of the imbalance.

Relieving Imbalance

Imbalance can result in our lives due to various reasons. When trying to determine the source, remember that the universe exists in a duality of forms, meaning that there are always two sides of the coin that must be viewed. So imbalance can come from a lack of attunement with the forces at hand or it can come from an over-abundance of the forces at hand.

In addition to this, there are three possible ways that these imbalances can come into being. The first is from the person's inner conflicts, the second is from outside influences from people and spirits, and the third can come from lack of attunement with the deities or elements. Below is a list of common sources that can lead a client to become unbalanced followed by the corresponding solution to that problem.

Source: Lack of attunement with your ancestral line.
Solution: Leave offerings of flowers or objects of affection on the graves of those relatives that have passed on.

Source: Lack of attunement with home and natural environment.
Solution: Perform a house cleansing ritual and spend time cleaning up your yard or home. Take a day away from friends and family and do things that have needed to be done.

Source: Conflicts between the mind and the emotions.
Solution: This is a common problem with the majority of people who come to me. When dealing with emotions, there is always confusion. First, you must see if the person is out of tune with the god or goddess of love. If this is the case, then offerings must be made to that deity in order to bring balance. If the imbalance is from an inner conflict, then a series of cleansing and spiritual baths to calm the mind must be performed.

Source: Lack of attunement with your patron deity or deities.
Solution: Offerings to the deities will solve this problem.

Source: Obstructions caused by the elemental spirits.
Solution: First you must find out what elements are out of balance and then perform a series of baths to balance the elements within. If there is a lack of fire energy, you would bathe in a fire bath. If there is too much fire, you would bath in a water bath to effect balance. The same applies for the other elements.

18

Source: Conflicts coming from negative energy projected to you from a man or a woman.

Solution: Reversing candles and a seven-day series of spiritual cleansing baths will solve the problem. (See Concerning Candles, chapter 6, and chapter 7 Spiritual Baths.)

Source: Lack of personal hygiene and/or health.

Solution: A diet consisting of fruits and vegetables for one week. No caffeine, very little meat, and daily cleansing baths for one week will eliminate any problems.

CONCERNING THE TENETS OF THE CRAFT

For many people coming into the craft, its many different aspects are overwhelming. When I am approached by prospective members of our coven, I talk with them and try to discern their reasons for wanting to be part of the craft. Experience has shown me that the majority of people coming into the craft enter it with the hopes of learning spells, potions, and magick. However, to these people I simply say that magical ability comes to each of us differently, and it is not handed out equally.

The powers of a witch come not through spells, but through attunement with nature. That attunement comes through living the way. Living the way begins with the basic tenets of the craft. These tenets are the core of how you are supposed to live.

Below is a list of the tenets in the form of positive affirmations. These should be read daily. It is important to remember that these tenets are not commandments. If you fail to live up to one or the other once in a while, you are not damned forever. Witchcraft, as a religion, does not promise power to anyone; it only promises a way of life. The tenets are our safeguard so that we do not bring unnecessary bad karma to ourselves (see Concerning Reincarnation and Karma, chapter 3).

TENETS OF THE CRAFT

- Today I will live a balanced life.
- Today I will live in harmony with everything and everyone.
- Today I will learn to trust and be worthy of the same.
- Today I will be humble.
- Today I will be tolerant of other faiths.
- Today I will learn something new.
- Through reincarnation, I have achieved the life that I live today, and constantly create what I will be in the next.
- Today I accept responsibility for my karma, which I create and recreate, as I constantly pursue the achievement of spiritual perfection.

CONCERNING THE THIRTEEN SPIRITUAL LAWS

Many schools of occult study teach that there are nine basic spiritual laws that we, as part of the vast creation, are subject to and cannot escape from. However, in keeping with the ways of witchcraft, I have included here thirteen spiritual laws.

1. *Law of Orderly Trend* - This law states that there is order in creation. All things that happen do so according to an organized plan. There are no "accidents" or "chance happenings" in the world. While this law does not prohibit us from exercising our free will, it does tend to move us in the direction of our destiny. We can choose to fight that destiny, but that will only lead to a stale or unhappy lifestyle.

2. *The Law of Polarities* - This law makes the statement that within all of creation everything has its equal but opposite. There cannot be positive without negative, up without down,

light without dark, left without right, and so on. This law is directly connected to the Law of Balance. Christianity believes that good and evil are in constant battle. Good and evil are human concepts created to try to explain hardship and pain by giving it a form upon which blame can be placed. The witch understands that what Christians view as good and evil are merely the opposite poles of the same thing. They coexist side by side. Without positive, the world would destroy itself. Without negative, the world would become overgrown and suffocate. Both are needed for the continuance of life.

3. *The Law of Balance* - This law states that all things in the universe seek for balance. Balance is the key to success and abundance. Just as water always seeks its lowest point and then levels off, so do our spirits seek for the highest point, where we can be reunited with that energy from which we came, i.e., god and goddess. Anything that brings us out of balance interferes with our true path and brings misfortune. Many schools of thought place this law and the Law of Opposites together as one law.

4. *The Law of Opulence* - This law stipulates that things attract unto themselves other things of the same type. In other words, like attracts like. It is by this law that much of the magick that witches perform works. Love attracts love; money attracts money; power attracts more power. Therefore, when working magick, use the actual objects, or symbols of them, that you wish to acquire. This type of magick is called sympathetic magick.

5. *The Law of Rebound* - This law tells us that a superior force always rebounds a lesser force. Therefore, if you, as a witch, come up against an opponent of lesser power who is using

negative magick against you, his negative will rebound on him, with both his own force as well as yours. The same is true if you try to use magick on someone greater than you.

6. *The Law of Cyclicity* - The Law of Cyclicity states that all things that exist are subject to cycles. All things return to the source from which they originated. The witch is especially tied into the Law of Cycles through the celebration of the wheel of the year and the cycles of the moon. By attuning ourselves to the cycles of nature, we place ourselves in tune with the universe and thereby make ourselves storehouses of universal energy and able to generate more power.

7. *The Law of Cause and Effect* - This law teaches us that all actions are caused by something, and every action has an effect that results from it. This is the Law of Three in its purest form. If we perform an action that causes a result, that result inextricably causes an effect—by the Law of Analogy—that influences all of creation. Also, by the Law of Cycles, that effect, whether positive or negative, will return to us in the end.

8. *The Law of Analogy* - This law states that we have correspondence and agreement regarding all forms in the universe. Everything is connected beyond separation. To affect one thing is to affect all things. To know one thing is to know all things. This law is the essence of the saying: "To know yourself is to know everything."

9. *The Law of Challenge* - This law tells us that anything that we come upon in the universe that does not appear to be logical or orderly should be challenged. Do not be trapped into false beliefs or false truths. Just because something is accepted by the majority of people around you does not make it truth. While all religions contain a spark of truth, no doctrine is

absolute truth (and yes, this includes Wicca). Question all that speaks against your knowledge and spirit.

10. *The Law of Change* - Everything is subject to change. Nothing in the universe is constant. Thus, being as all things are constantly in a state of perpetual changing, everything both is and is not.

11. *The Law of Triplicity* - This law tells us that all requests or chants should be repeated three times for maximum power. Three is a sacred number that is naturally magical. Throughout our history, the number three has been sacred. There are three fates, triple goddesses, three wishes from the genie, three little pigs, and so on.

12. *The Law of Opposites* - This law tells us that when we take something to its extreme it becomes its opposite. We cannot see in total darkness, but if a light is too bright and shining directly in our eyes, we are just as blind as being in darkness. A good example of this can be seen when police officers who become obsessed with catching "bad guys" begin to falsify evidence in order to arrest them. They have become a criminal by trying to catch a criminal. A saying that best describes this law is, "When one becomes obsessed with the enemy, one becomes the enemy."

13. *The Law of Equality* - When two forces meet and are of equal power, one will eventually give way to the other, which then rises in status. This can be seen when two groups of people meet or merge. Each group may have a leader, but when they combine, one leader will eventually take over both groups, with the other leader becoming second in command. This does not mean one is better than the other, only that one is more capable of handling a larger group.

Much meditation and thought can be given on these spiritual laws, and I recommend that you sit and contemplate the truth of all of these. By doing this, you will bring them into a better understanding. Living with the knowledge of these laws will allow you to go through life with no stress or guilt. These laws are valuable beyond comprehension and should be thoroughly read and understood.

CHAPTER 3

THE WITCH'S WORLD

And both to the Greeks and the Romans, to the
Assyrians and the Akkadians, the witch is a
member of society, and an integral element in the
communal fabric...

—HARRY WEDECK, *A TREASURY OF WITCHCRAFT*

CONCERNING COVEN STRUCTURE AND PRACTICES

If you are practicing alone, then there will be little need for you to worry about how a coven is structured. For those of you in an existing coven, you may find this information a little different than what your coven structure is, but most of it should seem familiar. I have included this section as a guide for those who are considering forming a coven and also to clarify some of the terminology used later on in this book.

The word *coven* comes from the Latin word *convenire*, which means "to come together." This is also the root of the words *convene, convention,* and, of course, *convent*. This tells you the real meaning behind a coven. A coven is a group of people who come together to worship, learn, and teach.

In the old days, a coven would only get together on the full moon and/or new moon for ritual. The rest of the month the witches were on their own and performed their magical experiments. When the time came for the coven to gather, they would meet in the woods or some other secret place and share the results of their experiments with their fellow witches. This is how the knowledge was passed on.

The meeting places for the Sabbats were never in the same place but rotated about so as to prevent detection and secure privacy. Some witches developed very cunning ways of letting the other witches know where the meeting was to take place. The one I like best is the coin. The witches would have several places that they would meet, and each one they associated with a specific coin. For example, you might attribute a quarter to a certain cave, a penny to the eastern edge of the woods and a dime to the western edge of the woods. On the coin would be scratched a certain symbol to let the witches know whom it came from. Three days prior to the meeting the witches would find the corresponding coin on their doorstep or somewhere near their home. Depending on which coin they found, they knew exactly where the meeting was to take place.

I have in my possession several English farthings dating back to the 1800s, each etched with a pentagram. Today, covens tend to meet on a more regular basis, and this is usually initiated by a phone call, although the coin method would add a nice sense of mystery. It is our coven's practice to meet every week for classes and circle.

In a coven, there is a certain hierarchy or chain of command that is followed. Below are titles that are given to certain members of the coven.

Priestess - The priestess acts as a spiritual guide to the members of the coven and oversees the rituals, training, and examination of those members just coming into the coven with the aid of the priest. The priestess, during ritual, is responsible for invocations of the goddess and is the representation of the female forces residing in nature. In witchcraft, women are treated with reverence and respect of highest order. This is often something that is very difficult for male beginners in the craft, especially if they come from a Christian background.

Priest - The priest is the male counterpart to the priestess, and his duties are the same as those of the priestess. The best arrangement is to have the priest and priestess together as a married couple. The priest representing the male forces of nature and the priestess representing the female. The closeness of the priest and priestess, and the entire coven for that matter, is vital to the success of coven rituals and spells. The priest acts as the medium for invocations of the god and as such is treated with the same respect as the priestess.

Maiden - This is a female assistant to the priestess. The maiden becomes the priestess's closest companion, and in the instance where the priestess is not able to perform a function within a ritual, the maiden will take her place. Such an instance will usually come when the priestess has invoked the goddess and cannot recite the words of the ritual. The maiden would then take over the recital to continue the ritual without conflict.

Fetch - This is the male equivalent of the maiden. The fetch acts as the priest's personal assistant and fills in for the priest should he be unable to attend or perform a function within the ritual, such as during invocations of the god. The name *fetch* comes from his duties of running errands for the coven and the priest and/or priestess. If you were to use the coin method of notifying members of a meeting, then it would be the fetch's job to place the coins at the houses of the various coven members.

These four positions are not necessary to have a working coven, as many times covens are simply two or three people. But as the coven grows, the priest and priestess will need help keeping things organized and training new initiates, thus the maiden and fetch become almost a necessity over time. I would recommend, however, that the coven hold off new memberships once the traditional thirteen members have been initiated. As members move up in the ranks, new persons can be initiated. This allows a more personal relationship to develop among the members. Close personal relationships cannot properly develop if the coven is too large.

The positions of priest, priestess, maiden and fetch can be rotated as the coven sees fit, provided that the position is held by someone who is qualified to carry that title. A maiden and fetch should be of at least first-degree standing, with full knowledge of the Sabbat rituals and circle casting. The priest or priestess must be of third-degree standing, with at least five years experience in ritual aspects and craft knowledge.

The degrees of initiation used in witchcraft simply determine a member's progress in their studies of the craft. Most covens use a three-tier system, meaning that there are three degrees of advancement.

A person showing interest in joining is usually made to wait a year and one day, during which he or she meets periodically with the various members of the coven. After that time, the coven decides whether or not the person should be initiated. If the decision is a yes, the new member is brought in and initiated into the first degree, and training begins. After the new member has proven that he or she has absorbed a certain amount of knowledge and acquired a certain amount of skill in the craft, a second initiation is performed and the person becomes a second-degree witch. Finally, after advancing a great deal, the second-degree witch is ready to become a priest or priestess and is given the third-degree initiation. Now the witch can stay and act as a teacher to new members or separate from the coven and form his or her own.

Once again, this is the most common form of structure but by no means the only form. The coven that I was originally initiated into had a three-tier system but did not require a year and a day waiting period, and new members were initiated right away. I do not recommend this method, because it hinders the family structure of the coven when total strangers are allowed into the coven to witness and participate in the rites, especially magical rites.

The second coven I joined, which was run by a so-called "authority" had only one degree. You were initiated right away and advanced at your own pace. This is not so bad, but it lacks the gradual climb and sense of achievement that a three-tier system gives.

I prefer a four-tier system of advancement. In this system, you have a dedication ritual, where the new members dedicate themselves to the study of the craft. They are then taught the basics of the craft for a year and a day. Provided they have absorbed the basics, they are then given their first-degree initiation, then second, and finally third.

These are just a few examples to give you an idea of how different groups can work. In the end, it is more important to follow your instincts as far as what the coven structure should be like. What works for one group will not necessarily work for all others.

CONCERNING REINCARNATION AND KARMA

Reincarnation is the process of living and dying and being reborn. But what exactly does this whole process encompass, and how does it fit into the religion of witchcraft? In the craft, we are taught the Law of Cyclicity, i.e., that all things in the universe run in cycles.

A physical manifestation of this law can be found throughout nature. The oxygen cycle, which we learn about in our early years of schooling, tells us that plants and trees breathe in carbon dioxide and breathe out oxygen. This oxygen is then breathed in by humans and animals who in turn breathe out carbon dioxide, which the plants then breathe in, and the cycle continues. Thus the existence of plants and animals is a cycle that is constantly repeated over and over again, and animal and plant life are dependent on each other.

In the cycle of water, we have rain that falls to the earth, is heated by the sun, and evaporates back into the sky, forming clouds again and eventually raining back down to the earth. These cycles are visible manifestations of the Law of Cyclicity. Both reincarnation and karma work in accordance with this Law.

When we die, our spirits rise (like water vapor) to a higher state of being. This higher state of being is of a spiritual nature and not at all physical. We rejoin with the forces and energies of our ancestors as well as the energies that created us (like clouds), and eventually we descend back to Earth in spirit and are implanted into a fetus to be reborn into the world (like rain). Thus the cycle of reincarnation works. It is a natural law and not simply a belief.

The concept of an eternal afterlife is totally unnatural, just as is the belief in no afterlife. Nature teaches us that every ending is but a beginning. Therefore the end of our physical life is just the beginning of our new spiritual life. To truly understand this is to remove the fear of death and what lies beyond and to open the way to true inner peace. Much meditation on the truth of this matter will bring you to the highest peaks of spirituality. So, if reincarnation is a fact of life (and death), then what is our purpose for being here? Quite simply, to learn and to do our part in the betterment of life as a whole. We are all individuals, yet by the Law of Analogy we are connected to everything and everyone, and thus we are also partially responsible for what happens to the world as a whole. Witchcraft, perhaps more than any other religion, is a religion of responsibility.

Karma is often discussed as going hand in hand with reincarnation and, indeed, the two do work together more often than not.

Karma is a Sanskrit word that means "action," but the actual functioning of karma is far more complex than that. Karma is primarily a combination of the Spiritual Laws of Cause and Effect and the Law of Cyclicity. A secondary function of karma is the Law of Balance.

It is a common belief that Karma operates almost as a cosmic checkbook of good and bad deeds. On one side we have our bad deeds listed and on the other side we have our good deeds listed. When our lives are over, this checkbook determines if we reincarnate under good or bad conditions, depending on how we lived our lives, and it also determines what debts are still owed.

Say, for example, a friend has done you a tremendous favor by letting you move in with her for two years while you finish college, and you die before being able to return that favor. In your next lifetime, or one much later on, you would be required, in some way or another, to return that favor, even if you do not remember the reason why or even know the person. That friend may be a homeless person in a future life, and upon seeing her you would feel compelled to help her by taking her into your home and cleaning her up.

Also, if you lived a life where you physically abused people or perhaps considered yourself more beautiful than others and constantly insulted people based on their physical appearance, you might reincarnate as a deformed person or a handicapped person in order to teach you the lesson of humility.

Some people believe that you can reincarnate as lesser animals and insects and even rocks. While I do not discount this theory, I can say that in the many years that I have practiced the method of bringing past-life memories to the surface, never has anyone told me that they were a tree, rock, or animal. This is not to say that it is not possible, however.

The above explanation of karma and how it works is a very simplistic view and does not cover the full scope of what karma is.

Karma, as stated earlier, has a secondary function as the Law of Balance. Karma constantly seeks to balance out the many lifetimes of actions that we have taken. Therefore it is a force that permeates our lives in every aspect. But it is erroneous to think that we only pay for our deeds in the next lifetime. If Karma can dispense of the debt in our current lifetime, it does. The only debts that carry over to other lives are the ones that we are unable to pay before dying in this incarnation.

Remember the Law of Cycles: all things return to the source from which they came. Every action that we do, whether good or bad, returns to us in the end, and not even death can stop it. Use the powers wisely and with good intention and you will be blessed threefold for it. Use the powers for selfish and foolish reasons and you will be cursed threefold.

CONCERNING THE TRIPLE DIVISION OF THE WORLD

> Seeing there is a threefold world . . .
>
> —AGRIPPA, *THREE BOOKS OF OCCULT PHILOSOPHY*

The craft often classes the world into three separate parts. These are called Upper World, Middle World, and Underworld.

The Upper World consists of the heavens—planets, stars, the Moon, and anything associated with higher powers. This realm also includes the astral plane and it is the realm of deities such as Zeus, Odin, Hera, Aphrodite, Hermes, as well as the spirits called Lare or Lasa.

The Middle World is often called Middle Earth, as it is the planet upon which we live. Middle Earth consists of the Earth, the forests, cities, and oceans. It is filled with the most diverse forms of any plane.

Spirits of the elements (gnomes, sylphs, undines, and salamanders) inhabit this plane, as well as all other planes. Also on this plane are the spirits known as fairies.

The Underworld is the realm of the dead. This is not to be looked upon as a dark and dismal place, although it does consist of places that fit this description. The Underworld is to be viewed just as Middle Earth. There are very beautiful places and there are also places that are very scary. This is the realm of deities such as, Hades, Hekate, the Furies, and the Harpies.

The triple division of the world as used by pagans and witches alike differs from the general view of many other belief systems, which view the Earth as the lowest level of existence possible. The triple division of the world is a more balanced view and coincides with the Law of Balance as well as the Law of Triplicity.

CONCERNING THE FIVE ELEMENTS OF CREATION

All that exists, exists as a combination of the elements. These elements of creation stem back into the ancient philosophies of the Greeks and Romans. They are Earth, Air, Fire, Water, and Spirit.

When dealing with the elements, it is important that you keep in mind that we are not speaking of the actual element itself, but rather the qualities or principles of that element. For example, although soil has a predominance of Earth energy infused into it, it is not pure Earth energy. Therefore, we look to the qualities of the element to find the hidden power behind it. Each element has within itself a constructive (active) quality and a destructive (passive) quality. Also, each element has a specific quality that can best be described as either electric or magnetic. Meaning that the energy of the element either moves outward, or draws inward.

The topic of the elements has often been discussed in a rather undermining way, implying that it is simple and basic knowledge. In reality, the interaction of the elements in the physical and spiritual worlds is the most complex and fascinating study and practice that any witch could hope to have. Let us take each element in turn and fully explain the qualities and principles associated with it.

The Element of Spirit

All of the elements of creation, Fire, Water, Air and Earth, originated from the Etheric Principal, or the element of Spirit. Spirit is often called the fifth power, but in actuality it is the first power. The element of Spirit is ultimate, supreme, and unconceivable. Spirit is spaceless and timeless. Many ceremonial magicians refer to it as the "unmanifest universe," many religions attach the name "God" to it. However, we as humans cannot truly understand the Spirit element.

The best way to describe it is to give a brief analogy. Suppose for example that you wanted to build a table. You gather up the wood, the nails, the glue, and the tools to build it and throw them all together in a pile. Now say that you could melt all of those materials and mix them together into one substance. This substance would have everything in it that a table is made of but would not actually be a table. This is what the element of Spirit is.

Spirit contains within itself the substance of every thing that exists, but is nothing in and of itself. I know, it is confusing, but if it were not, then it would not be Spirit. I often describe Spirit as an infinite pool of light that is conscious of its existence but contains no actual form. This description, however, is intrinsically inaccurate, because Spirit is indescribable, and any attempt to label or describe it puts limitations on it and thereby becomes an inaccurate description. Spirit creates and destroys because that is its nature, but it does not think or understand why it does this. Christianity tries to view Spirit as God. But to limit Spirit by giving it a gender or imparting it a personality negates the true nature of Spirit and results in confusion.

The Element of Fire

Fire was the first element that sprang from the element of Spirit, and thus it is the closest in quality to spirit. Fire's power is electric and expanding. Fire energy radiates outward, affecting everything it touches.

In its constructive sense, Fire is enlightening, warming, and expansive. In its destructive sense, Fire is consuming, burning, and deadly. Fire cannot be contained, but it can be controlled. It has the freedom of Spirit and is the activating principle in everything that exists. No other element initiates action on its own without the direct influence of the Fire element.

Physical fire is the representation of this power as it manifests on the physical plane. This is interesting, because physical fire is somewhat of an enigma. It can be seen and felt, but, in essence, it does not exist of itself. The flames of a fire are not actually physical; they are a result of a chemical breakdown of the elements that are burning. Thus fire is also purifying.

The Element of Water

In accordance with the Law of Balance, the element of Water was the second element to spring from Spirit. Water is the polar opposite of Fire. While Fire's basic qualities are heat and expansion, Water's basic qualities are cold and constriction. Water energy is magnetic and receptive. Water can be contained and stored away. It is moveable and easily controlled when it is not combined with other elements.

In the example of a tidal wave, water is very destructive and uncontrollable, but in order for the tidal wave to happen it is usually acted on by the element of fire, i.e., volcanic eruptions or earthquakes. The positive qualities of Water are those of cleansing, soothing, and life giving. In its negative aspect, Water is corrosive, dissecting, and stagnant.

The Element of Air

The element of Air resulted from the combination of Fire and Water. When Fire and Water met, a great pillar of steam arose and created the element of Air. It is because of this that Air's quality is neither electric nor magnetic but is actually neutral. Air can be felt, but not seen. Air can be contained and stored away.

Air's primary duty is acting as the mediator of Fire and Water. It is the balancing element and thus contains aspects of both fire and water. From Fire, it has acquired the quality of warmth and from Water it has acquired moisture. In its positive role, Air is life giving, refreshing, and mentally stimulating. On the negative side, air is stale, changeable, and erratic.

The Element of Earth

Out of the interaction of the previous three elements, the element of Earth arose. In essence, the first three condensed and formed the element Earth, which is the heaviest and thus the most material of the five elements. Being as Earth contains all of the other elements within it, its Power is electromagnetic.

The element Earth is both the place of birth, for all life comes from the earth, and the place of death, for all life decomposes and returns to its basic elements. In its positive sense, Earth is fertile, stable, and life giving. On its negative side, Earth is suffocating, restrictive, and consuming.

Analyzing the Elements

Everything that exists, both physical and spiritual, can be categorized according to these five basic elements. To truly understand this, look to the world around you and see the operation of the elements in everything you see. Analyze each aspect of the elements and see them interacting with each other to create our world.

For example, anything that is solid will have a predominance of Earth element. If something is a forged metal, such as a knife, it will have Earth energy, but it will be predominantly Fire, because of the forging process. Remember, Fire purifies and removes, activates or negates the effects of all other energy. If something is liquid, then the predominant energy is Water. If something is light and wispy, like a feather, then Air is abundant in it. Flammable liquids such as alcohol or gasoline would be a combination of Water and Fire energy in near perfect balance.

Look about you and dissect the world into its elemental parts; then you will begin to see how and why the world works and lives. Do the same with people. A person who is quick tempered will have a predominance of Fire energy, a dreamy person will have too much Air, an overly emotional person too much Water, and a lazy person too much Earth.

CHAPTER 4

THE EIGHT WAYS
OF MAKING MAGICK

And the number Eight is sacred to the Witch, for there be Eight Sabbats, Eight Working Tools, and Eight Ways of Making Magick.

—LORD CORVUS OF THESSALY, *BOOK OF SHADOWS*

In traditional witchcraft, there are eight methods that a witch can use to raise magical power. These eight ways of making magick have been listed by various authors, but few have ever discussed fully how to use them. Some authors have even changed them to make them more "politically correct," which is, in my opinion, ridiculous and idiotic, but more on that later. Magical power is raised by using one or more of these methods and then sent through to its target by the use of symbols or links. In this chapter I will discuss each of these methods and show how to incorporate them into your craft.

METHOD 1: CONCENTRATION

How many books have you read that say that concentration is the key to successful magick? Plenty. How many of those books have actually explained how to develop your concentration abilities? Not many.

Concentration is an aspect of our mental faculties that few Westerners ever master completely. The ability to focus the attention on one thing, without interruption or derivation, is the single most important faculty any human being can achieve, be they witch, ceremonialist, priest, priestess, or layperson. So how do you develop this most wonderful ability? Well, as with anything else: practice, practice, practice!

Developing Concentration

Step 1. The first step to developing concentration is to set aside five minutes a day in which you will be undisturbed. Unplug the phone, lock the doors, turn off your pager, try to remove any other possible source of distractions, and sit down in an armless chair with your palms resting in your lap and your feet flat on the ground. Burn some sandalwood incense and for five minutes let your mind run wild. Just let your thoughts flow from one to the other.

Five minutes may not seem long, but after about two minutes you will start looking to the clock to see how much longer you have left. Try to fight the urge to look at the clock. In fact, I have found the best thing to use is a cooking timer, available at any grocery store. I prefer the digital clocks to the wind-up timers so the constant ticking does not distracted me. Simply set the timer to go off in five minutes, close your eyes, and follow your thoughts.

At first, your mind will be filled with a wide array of thoughts. No doubt you will be thinking of how this exercise is working; this may then progress into thoughts of future progress on the witch's path; then you may go into thoughts of the day's previous events, then perhaps into the past a little further or maybe the distant future. In any case, let your thoughts go. Do not analyze them; just let them go.

After about three to four minutes you will find that you are more than likely repeating the same pattern of thoughts. This is good. Make a note of your experiment in your journal and repeat the exercise the following day, but on the second day you should increase the time to six minutes. Keep this up until you have reached a total elapsed time of ten minutes. Thus if you start on a Monday with the five-minute session, by Saturday your session should last ten minutes.

Step 2. For this next step in the progress toward better concentration, you will follow the same directions as you did in step one, but when you have completed the required time for the session, you will remain seated and mentally retrace your thoughts. For example, say that, after five minutes, you were thinking of driving to work, but your first thought was about your leaky faucet in the kitchen. Take that last thought of driving to work and trace your thoughts back to the leaky faucet. How did you go from thinking of the leaky faucet to thinking about driving to work? Analyze your thought process. Your last thought was about driving to your job, the one prior to that was in regards to your vehicle, which had gotten wet inside because you left the window down in a rainstorm a few months ago, the thought prior to that was about your dishes needing to be washed, which lead to the beginning thought of the leaky faucet.

Now that you have it figured out, rethink it again. You began by thinking of your leaky faucet, which led you to think about your dishes that need to be washed. This thought in turn led to think about the rainstorm during which you left your vehicle window down and got the interior wet, which in turn led you to think about driving to work.

I know this seems redundant, but by doing this exercise you will break down your thinking process and get a better understanding of how your own mind thinks and operates. By getting a better understanding of this, you will better understand how to control and regulate those thoughts. Begin this exercise with a five-minute session and increase the time by one minute each day until you reach ten minutes.

Step 3. By the time you reach this step, you should have a firm grip on the processes your mind uses to think and analyze. If you feel that you have not fully mastered these techniques, continue practicing the exercises until you do. For this third step, you will do as you did in the two previous steps, but instead of letting your thoughts go wild for the whole length of time, you should focus only on the first thought in your mind. So whatever comes to mind first, that is the thought you should have at the end. No other thoughts at all.

A useful tool, that I might suggest, to help mark your progress in this step is to have fifty or so small beads or seeds in a small cup and hold this cup in your hand. Each time your thoughts move from the original thought, place one bead down on the floor or table in front of you and bring your thought back to the original one. If you run out of beads before the time is up, then you know that your mind is definitely out of control!

Remember, for the most part your thoughts have probably had free reign in your life. Your mind and thoughts must be disciplined like a small child to get them under control. Continue this exercise until you can hold one thought for a full ten minutes without interruption or with relatively few interruptions. This will take some time, and as with the other steps, I suggest you gradually work up from five minutes to ten minutes. But this time, do not increase by one minute each day; rather, persist until you have been able to hold the thought for the full allotted time.

Step 4. This step is a natural move forward from Step 3. In this step you will force your mind to think of something that it does not want to. Look about the room you are in and locate an object: a clock, pencil, chair, anything. This will be the object of concentration. Think only of the object. Do this until you can hold the object in your mind for a full ten minutes.

When you have completed these exercises and can hold any thought or object in your mind for a full ten minutes, you will have phenomenal powers of concentration and upon beginning any work of magick, will have most of the work completed before you even begin.

METHOD 2:
INVOCATIONS, SPELLS, AND CHANTS

I will discuss each of these techniques separately; however, in actual practice chants, spells, and invocations are used simultaneously to perform magick.

Invocations

> *You also, O Moon, I draw down from the Heavens . . .*
>
> —MEDEA, WITCH OF THESSALY

Most Witches are quite familiar with the terms "drawing down the Moon" and "drawing down the Sun." For those of you just coming in, let me explain these terms more closely. Drawing down the Moon is the term used when a priest calls the goddess to descend in spirit and take over the thoughts and actions of the priestess. Drawing down the Sun is when the priestess calls the god to descend in spirit and take over the thoughts and actions of the priest. The technical occult terminology for this act of magick is called *invocation*.

One thing that I find just amusing to no end is the idea put forth in many books on the craft that the priest or priestess invokes the deity and then is given special lines to read to the coven. Would you invite a guest speaker to your group and then force him or her to read a speech you prepared? How rude! These types of invocations, for the most part, are merely acting.

Of course, it is possible to summon the energy of a deity so that the priest or priestess vibrates with the energy of that god or goddess and still maintains his or her own personality, but a true invocation is the complete letting go to the deity and allowing the deity to function within the person for a short time. When this is done, the person invoking is no longer the individual you knew, but is now a deity in flesh. Therefore, you should not be surprised when he or she goes off and does something that is not part of the written ceremony. After all, would you argue with a god or goddess who decided to lead the coven in dance and song rather than meditation? Learn from the deity and learn from the experience.

Let me first give you the standard warning. Any invocation, even of the friendliest deities, is not without its dangers. These dangers are not physical, but rather mental and spiritual and can come when one confuses one's personality with that of the god or goddess who has been invoked. Persons who may have suffered from mental disorders such as schizophrenia, multiple-personality disorder, or paranoia should be especially careful when performing invocations.

How is this strange process of invocation accomplished? Performing invocations is much easier than many people think it is. To begin with, you must know as much about the deity you are invoking as you possibly can. Learn their likes and dislikes. Then you should surround yourself with as much of their attributes and associations as possible.

Let us say, for example, that you wished to invoke the goddess Athena. After some research, you learn that her sandals and helmet were two very consistent images associated with her. Also, the owl is sacred to her, as is the olive tree. Therefore, when performing your rite, you would want to surround yourself with as many of these objects as possible. A drawing of her, perhaps photocopied out of a book, would be excellent, a statue even better. At the foot of this image, place offerings of olives (black olives), perhaps a photo of an owl, and some gold sandals.

Research is the primary key to effective invocations. Once you have the information and the materials at hand, you simply call the deity to you. All of the associations and imagery act as a direct link to the power and spirit of whatever deity they are attributed to. This link is absolutely necessary for a successful invocation. The more ancient an image is, the more people have prayed to and worked with that image, the better a link it will be to that power. Thus, museum replicas of statues of deities are extremely effective for use in invocations. (See Concerning the Use of Statues for Worship, chapter 6.)

The actual invocation is performed by constantly repeating a request for the deity to descend into the priest, priestess, or yourself. While this request is being repeated, the person invoking the deity must focus entirely on the presence of the deity, concentrating and feeling the deity descend and step into the person, as though stepping into a suit of clothing. The entire process, when done correctly, may take only a few minutes.

When you first begin, it can take up to an hour for any good results. Mark your progress by the feelings and ideas that spring into your mind. If you get a sudden flash of the chills and a slight mental disorientation, then you are doing quite well. It is very difficult for your mind to completely let go and allow another entity to take over.

I often ask others if they are aware of their surroundings when they are "ridden" by a god or goddess. I, for one, am not. When I perform an invocation of a deity for my students or for myself, I am usually unconscious of the time, place, and surroundings; yet somehow I remember the information the deity wanted me to know. However, I have great difficulty remembering what the deity has said to others. I know all of this sounds a bit on the fantastic side, but if you have ever experienced a true invocation, whether you invoked the deity or watched as someone else did, you will never forget the experience.

Let me share with you an excerpt from my personal journal regarding an invocation I performed of the god Dionysus.

> . . .*after consuming a large quantity of wine, I began to feel the presence of Dionysus around me. In fact, I remember going outside to the coveners sitting there and telling them that I felt him close by. I channeled this energy through me and projected it out through my hands as I passed my palms near some of the coveners' heads and faces. The male coveners immediately felt disoriented and giddy. The female coveners were immediately sexually aroused by the energy and asked me to stop. I returned to my chamber and proceeded to ask Dionysus to enter into me. I remember feeling his presence standing over me from behind and it felt as though he had dove into my mind. I do recall a sweet smell, like candy, then all went blank. This invocation was a little unusual for me, because unlike the others, I remember fragments of what happened once Dionysus was within me. I distinctly remember touching several coveners and watching them suddenly filled with joy and excitement. This made me feel good. I wanted all of them to feel the joy that I was feeling now. Dionysus was apparently pleased with the gathering and the celebration. The next thing I recall was looking toward the goats in my neighbors yard and telling Dionysus, "We don't do that anymore." (A note to the reader: In ancient times, a goat or sheep was sacrificed to Dionysus.) Dionysus accepted this change with no fuss. I don't remember much else, other than when I became aware of a nausea in my*

stomach, obviously from the large consumption of wine. I returned to my chamber and was followed by Djinn (a male covener) and Anthony (a new prospect). . . . Dionysus wanted to remain with the celebration longer, so he jumped from me and entered into Djinn. From Djinn, he then jumped into Anthony, who had no idea what was going on. I found out later, that Anthony came back to his senses several hours later and several miles away from the celebration! He was aware of his surroundings the entire time, but his mind was somewhat detached and almost daze-like he told me later. (Church of Thessally's Festival of Dionysus, February 13, 1999)

This is an account of a true invocation and should serve also as a warning. While no one suffered any negative effects from this invocation, I shudder when I think of what could have happened to Anthony had Dionysus taken him fully.

Some of you out there may be asking why this invocation was not done within a circle? Well, it was. I had erected a circle in my chamber prior to the invocation, but for a great celebration with dozens of people present, a circle just would not be large enough. In ancient times, this type of invocation was done at every celebration dedicated to a deity. If there was not an actual person invoking the god or goddess, the deity was called down into a statue.

Spells

Whenever a person approaches me with questions about witchcraft, I can rest assured that the subject of spells will come into the conversation. This is perhaps the most alluring aspect of the craft to outsiders or those who are interested. Spells are filled with magick and mystery, and the witch always seems to know just what to do when a problem arises.

The magick of a spell works through the use of symbols, drawing on the theory that things that are similar are somehow connected. Thus if you name a candle after a certain person and place an object that belongs to that person in or under the candle, the candle will actually connect to that person, and whatever is done to the candle will happen to the person.

In essence, a spell is the symbolic representation of your will. To properly perform a spell, you gather objects that coincide with your desire, for example, pictures, writing, drawings, hair, fingernails, and so on, and you arrange those objects in a special way so that you can impose your will upon them. Doing this will bring change through the law of analogy. There are eight ways to raise power, and there are literally an infinite number of ways to work that power into a spell. Here is one example.

Spell to Open New Roads. When our lives seem to be stagnant and there is no movement, this simple little rite will bring swift changes for your benefit. It works on the level of believing that the roads you travel are no longer open for you to move forward.

ITEMS NEEDED

- Key (preferably the old-type round keys, but any key will do)
- Red ribbon

Tie the key with the red ribbon and hang it on your front door. As you hang it say the following:

> *By this key which I hang here,*
> *To bring good fortune near.*
> *Good fortune do I trust will be,*
> *Always close and near to me.*

Let the key hang there for one week and then take it to a place where two or more roads meet and tie it up there to "unlock" the roads. You can tie this to a street sign, a telephone pole, or a streetlight; anything that is there will do. If you can, do this without anyone seeing you. As you tie it up say:

> *The Roads are closed, but I hold the key*
> *To open all paths that lie before me.*
> *Swift changes come and with them they bring*
> *The best of fortune in everything.*

Turn and walk away and do not look back. The spell is done.

Concerning Chants

> *The central regions of Thessaly, are universally known for magic incantations.*
>
> —APULEIUS, ROMAN NOVELIST

Chants, or incantations, are a powerful means of raising and sending magical energy. A chant can be repeated over and over until the correct frame of mind is induced. This process is similar to hypnosis. Traditional witchcraft chants are short and rhythmic. The words of a chant should rhyme in order for the chant to be more effective.

In the different spells and rituals that I have included within this work, you will find a wide variety of chants. These should give you a good idea of how chants work and are composed. Rhyming chants are the only type that I use in magick, for the simple reason that they work better and are easily remembered. The mind also remains more easily focused on the task at hand. Chants are a matter of practice and trial and error. Just remember to keep them as short and rhythmic as possible.

METHOD 3: ASTRAL PROJECTION

Astral Projection can best be defined as the conscious separation of your spirit from your physical body, allowing you to travel uninhibited by the restrictions of the physical body. Not all witches can astral project.

In olden days, certain ointments were used to induce astral projection. The recipes for these "flying ointments" contain a wide array of herbs, mostly poisonous in nature. The recipes are still available, but I refrain from giving them here, as they can be very dangerous if misused. The old recipes never give exact amounts to use in these ointments, and so the chance of overdosing is greatly increased if one does not fully understand the use of herbs.

A much safer method of achieving astral projection is to attempt it during sleep. Prior to going to bed, anoint your forehead with sandalwood oil, as this oil vibrates in a way conducive to projection. Lie down comfortably in your bed, close your eyes and roll your eyes upward, as if trying to look up into your own skull. Now visualize a silver line issuing from your forehead and extending out above you for about four feet. Fix your attention on the end of that line. This will force you to place your conscious attention to a point outside of your body and will eventually lead to astral projection. Astral projection can be fun and also very useful. Experiment and you will see.

METHOD 4: POTIONS

In nearly all stories about witches, you will come across the word *potions*. Potions are the stock and trade of the witch. The word as I use it here includes many varied items, such as incense, magical anointing oils, herbal teas, ointments, and alcoholic beverages. The purposes of these potions are as varied as the ways in which they are prepared. A witch can use potions to heal, bring money, attract love, or even promote fertility.

The concoction of potions is a study that can take a lifetime. To make effective potions, several years of study are needed. It is best, when dealing with potions, to study under a trained elder who is knowledgeable in this area. Some potions, such as the infamous "flying ointment" used by witches, contain herbs that, if taken in the wrong amounts, can cause sickness and even death. I have, for the safety of the reader, not included these recipes. For those who wish to learn more about this information I would advise you to seek out a Wiccan elder who is willing to teach.

Potions can work either magically, that is, through the use of controlled energy, or medicinally, by incorporating the chemical compounds of plants for use as medicine. I discuss the medicinal use of herbs in potions in chapter 8 on herbs; likewise in chapter 9 on dreams, I discuss an herbal tea (potion) that will enhance your dreaming. In this chapter, I will discuss the use of magical waters used by witches and give an example of one.

Magical Waters

The use of magical waters draws on the magical quality of the Water element to absorb a "charge," or idea. Water's energy is magnetic, and it is because of that quality that water can be magically charged for any purpose that a witch intends.

Not all potions are a concoction of fifty herbs and oils and obscure objects collected from the far reaches of the globe. A simple glass of water can become a powerful magical spell simply by holding it and pouring your desire into it. This is sometimes called "magical impregnation"; however, I prefer the term "charging."

To charge the water, you sit or stand quietly with a bowl or glass of water in front of you. Look intently into the water and imagine a point floating in the center of the water. Now build up your desire and push the energy of that desire through your eyes and into that point in the center of the water.

It is not uncommon at this point to "see" an image of your desire appear in the water just as though you were gazing into a crystal ball. In fact, the Greeks favored the use of a bowl of water for gazing (or scrying as it is sometimes called) to that of crystals. Water is certainly easier to obtain and much cheaper.

Once you have poured your energy into the water you can take it and place it on a windowsill where the sun will hit it. As the water evaporates, your energy is released, and the spell will take effect.

To add additional power to your washes, you can first blend certain things into them and then charge them. For example, a tea made from mugwort herb increases psychic powers when you drink it. What if you took that tea and magically charged it with your intention and then drank it? That would certainly increase the potency and bring your goal to you that much sooner. Experiment and be creative.

Healing Water. I used this potion on myself once when I had surgery on my left arm, which was broken in an accident. For this wash, I simply charged the water for healing and added some blue food coloring, as blue is the color for healing. I drank the potion down in large quantities, without thinking about it. My arm healed at twice the normal speed the doctor had expected, and all went well.

I once gave a bottle of this same potion to a friend who also had a broken arm and wished for it to heal faster. I told him to take only a ½ cup a day, but he did not listen to me and guzzled the whole thing down in one day. Now, granted a healing potion such as this one will not cause any harm if too much is taken, but he did become disoriented and giddy. He also swears that for an entire year after taking the potion he never caught cold, flu, or any other sickness.

METHOD 5: DANCING

Dancing has always played an important role in the magick of the ancients. Who has not, at least once in their lives, been lost in a song and spontaneously broken into dance? Music and dancing is a wonderful way to raise power.

All you have to do is listen to the music and allow the rhythm of the song to take over, and you will begin to move and dance. You should not be concerned with how silly the dance may look; let the gods and the spirits guide you, and the dance will be wonderful. When in circle, dancing should always be done deosil or clockwise, so as to bring in the flow of positive energy.

METHOD 6: CORD MAGICK

Beware of witches who blow upon knots!

—UNKNOWN AUTHOR

One of the most ancient practices of witchcraft is the use of cords in spell casting. Cord magick is quick, effective, and more diverse than it might first appear. The most common use of the magick cord is for binding spells, which are designed to hinder a person's influence over you or another person. But cords also can be used in love spells, prosperity spells, purification rites, and healing spells. (See Concerning Magical Cords, chapter 6, for a full discussion of cord magick.)

Upon your initiation into a coven, or if you are working solitary, your dedication, one of the first things you should do is make your first magick cord. This cord should be red in color (color of blood). In addition to this red cord you should also braid a black cord, a white cord, and one that is both black and white mixed together. This gives you a total of four cords to use in your magical spells.

Some witches like to use cords of the planetary colors, and this is also acceptable if you wish to do so. For these planetary colors you would have a total of seven cords: gold or orange (Sun), red (Mars), purple (Jupiter), white or yellow (Mercury), black (Saturn), green or pink (Venus), and silver or white (Moon).

The spell that you are casting will determine what colored cord to use. For works of a positive nature, such as healing, prosperity, and increase, you would use your red cord. For your works of spirituality you would use your white cord. When performing bindings to keep another person's influence out of your life, you would use your black cord. When making a witch's ladder, the black and white cords are the ones to use.

METHOD 7: THE SCOURGE

The scourge is a witch's tool that is steeped in controversy. Most modern traditions of the craft do not even use the scourge anymore, dismissing it as a nontraditional tool that is only used by people as a way to act out their own sadomasochistic desires, using religion as an excuse. This could not be any further from the truth. The scourge, if properly used, can be one of the most beneficial tools for a witch.

The scourge actually has two uses in witchcraft. Symbolically, the scourge represents purification and death. Thus in the myth of the descent of the goddess, the goddess descends to the realm of the Lord of Death and kneels to be scourged by him. This is symbolic of the removal of her former self and submission to the hand of Death, which inevitably leads to rebirth. Likewise, in the initiation of a witch, the initiate is bound and scourged as a symbol of his or her death. The binding is the restriction of the grave, and the scourging is the actual release of the spirit from the body. There have been cases where, during initiation, a prospect has spontaneously astral projected during the scourging.

The second use of the scourge is to induce trance states. This is a more complicated process and should not be performed unless fully understood. To induce trance, the person kneels on the floor while another witch begins to lightly scourge the person, aiming directly between the shoulder blades. The strokes should be steady and monotonous. Not so hard as to inflict pain, but hard enough to draw blood away from the brain and into the area being scourged. Results will be noticeable in a matter of minutes, as the person being scourged will become drowsy.

While this is taking place, the receiver of the scourging should be focusing on his or her goal. This goal can be anything from astral projection to communication with a deity or spirit. The important thing to remember is that once the vision starts the scourging should cease. This is a rather tricky thing to gauge, and that is why I do not suggest this be performed unless it is with a trained priest or priestess of the craft overseeing or performing it.

Self-flagellation or scourging oneself can be done with little danger, but this is not as effective, because when the trance state begins, the scourging would cease and thus only allow you to reach the lightest states of trance.

The scourge is one of the easiest tools to make. To start with, you will need a branch from an oak tree. The oak is a tree of protection and is considered the king of trees, thus it is a fitting wood to use for a tool that represents dominance and authority. The length of this branch should be 1 cubit (the length measured from your elbow to the tip of your middle finger); this will be the handle.

Now braid eight black cords, (see Concerning Magical Cords, chapter 6) each 1 cubit in length. Glue these eight cords around one end of the oak handle and then wrap leather straps around them to hold them in place.

There are no symbols that need to be placed on the scourge, but should your intuition guide you to place symbols on it, feel free to do so. Make certain, however, that these symbols coincide with the actual purpose behind the scourge: dominance, purification, and symbolic death. Once you have the cords secured onto the scourge, tie five knots in each of them.

This results in forty knots, and this is a sacred number in witchcraft. Numerologically, 8 x 5 = 40 (eight Sabbats; five elements). If we add the 8 and 5 we get 13, the witch's number. 40 = 4 + 0 = 4 (quarters and Watchers). There are many others numerological associations that go with the number 40, but I will leave those up to you, the reader, to figure out.

METHOD 8: THE GREAT RITE

This is the rite that is undoubtedly the most misunderstood rite of witchcraft. Certainly it is the source of much controversy, and many groups do not even teach the methods involved with the actual Great Rite but resolve to teach it only in symbolic form. The Great Rite is the Wiccan act of ritualized sexual intercourse, and it can be performed either in actuality or symbolically. To fully understand the symbolic Great Rite, one should first look at the actual rite and the reason that it is used.

Ritualized sexual intercourse between the priest and priestess of the coven is steeped in the ancient tradition of the *Hieros Gamos,* or sacred marriage. During this particular rite, the priestess would invoke the goddess and the priest would invoke the god. The two would then be ritually married and join in sexual union in order to bring fertility and prosperity to the land and the people. This was a very sacred rite and one that was crucial to the safety, well-being and continuation of the people. See chapter 12 for the description of how this rite is to be performed.

Sometimes, only the priest or priestess would invoke the deity and, as a "love offering," a young man or woman from the town would become the concubine of the deity. Here you may find the source for the many myths of gods and goddesses descending to Earth and begetting children. For during the act of conception, if a man or woman has invoked the deity, that energy would then carry into the child, thus giving birth to a very special human being. If the priest and priestess both invoke their respective deities, then the resulting child would be a god or goddess. Thus you find in classical mythology many stories of the births of gods and goddesses occurring in many different ways and in many different places.

CHAPTER 5

THE WITCH'S SYMBOLS: THE PENTAGRAM AND CIRCLE

Mephostopheles - "I must confess that forth I may not wander. My steps by one slight obstacle controlled - the Witch's-foot, that on your threshold is made." Faust - "So the pentagram prohibits Thee?"

—GOETHE, *FAUST*

CONCERNING THE PENTAGRAM

The pentagram, or five-pointed star, is so closely associated with witchcraft that the two have become almost synonymous. However, few witches realize that this symbol did not originate from our craft. The pentagram has been used from the earliest of times. Pythagoras, the ancient Greek philosopher, used the inverted pentagram as the symbol of his mystical order. To him the inverted pentagram symbolized spirit encased within physical matter.

Ceremonial magicians have long used the upright pentagram as the symbol of spirit ruling over matter. Each point of the pentagram represents one of the elements of creation. The placement of the elements on these points varies depending on which system of magick you are using. I have found, through my practices, that the order given below works best for my group and me.

This alignment of the elements is in accordance with the order of creation as depicted in the Church of Thessally. Following the points, starting from Akasha, and going clockwise, the order in which the universe was created is revealed.

First, there was Spirit, the infinite cosmos that has consciousness but not form. This Great Spirit was aware of itself, but could not conceive of its vastness; because it filled all space, there was not a point outside of itself from which it could view itself. Imagine trying to see yourself in a mirror that is located inside of your body. It cannot be done.

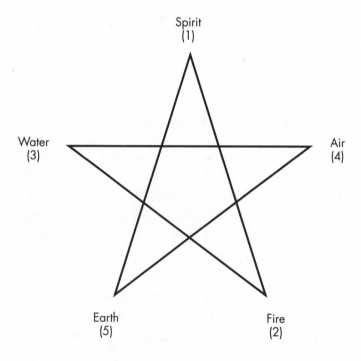

This condition caused Spirit to be confused. Just as our spirits seek to understand our selves and our world, so did this spirit seek to understand its greatness. But no matter where it searched, it found itself, causing a great deal of turmoil in Spirit.

It began to search inward, forming a spiral. This spiral turned faster and faster until all of Spirit became compressed into a great cosmic egg. Once this happened, Spirit looked out from this egg and saw the space it had once filled, which was infinity. At last, spirit understood its vastness, and the turmoil was gone. With no more tension, the egg exploded, and out poured an infinite number of stars, galaxies, and universes.

From the explosion, Fire was the first element born. As with any explosion, there is fire. Now, the Law of Opposites came into play. Everything that exists must have an equal opposite. So in order for Fire to not consume all that was there, Water was the second born. When Fire and Water met, a great pillar of steam arose, and the element of Air was created. As the great cosmic explosion cooled, the three elements condensed and the Element of Earth was created. This is the order of the creation of the elements.

This scenario is symbolic and should be viewed as a spiritual interpretation of the creation of the universe. Meditation on this aspect of the pentagram and what it represents can bring about very profound insights and ideas. So when you, as a witch, place a pentagram or pentacle on a chain and wear it about your neck, remember that it is not just a five-pointed star that you are wearing, but also the secrets of the universe itself!

CONCERNING THE USES OF THE PENTAGRAM

Due to its universal symbolism, the pentagram lends itself to many varied uses. For the witch, probably the two most common uses are for protection and for summoning the quarters.

In order for the pentagram, or any other symbol, to be used for protection, it needs to be fully understood. A symbol is only powerful if the person using it has full knowledge of what the symbol represents. So understanding that the pentagram represents the order of creation and thus contains all the powers of the universe within it can allow the witch to withstand any type of magical or spiritual attack or problem. Such protection can be brought about in various ways. Below is a protection ritual that I use in order to banish evil or negativity from a person's aura.

Pentagram Protection Ritual

Preliminary Work. Before this ritual is conducted, the client should be instructed to first take a purification bath to remove unwanted negative astral debris attached to his or her aura. This ritual will seal off the person's aura from psychic attack. If you do not remove the negativity already attached, you will only serve to seal it in, thus causing more problems for your client.

ITEMS NEEDED

- Stained-glass pentacle (can be bought through various occult catalogs)
- White tapered candle
- Dark room
- Bottle of Glory Water

The Operation. Have the client sit in a chair in the center of the room. Guide him through a relaxation meditation so that his mind is calm and his spirit is accepting. Light the tapered candle and circle around the client *counter clockwise* (to banish) three times while chanting:

Evil, Harm, Negativity
From thy life, banished be.

Next, take up the stained-glass pentacle in your right hand and with the other hand hold the taper directly behind it. This will project a colored-light pentacle onto the person. Move the candle back and forth until the pentagram is located on the person's face and say:

By power of the five-point star
I seal your aura from evil both near and far.

Move the projected image down to the throat and repeat the chant. Continue down to each of the power centers: heart, solar plexus, groin, and feet. When this is complete, the work is done and the person's aura is sealed from all negativity. The effects of the ritual are quite powerful.

As an added note, if you cannot find a stained-glass pentacle, you can substitute by using a regular pentacle from a necklace, only you would have the client lie down and you would dangle the pentacle directly over the power center, making it circle clockwise.

Using the Pentagram for Calling Down Power

The pentagram's most infamous use is in the summoning of spirits or powers. Nearly every witch is familiar with drawing these pentagrams in order to summon the Watchers (see Concerning the Watchers, chapter 11). This is done by using the index finger or wand and magically drawing, in the air before you, the shape of the pentagram. As an added note, the athame should be used only to banish a magical pentagram, and the wand or index finger used to invoke or summon. The reason for this is that the athame is a tool of defense and attack, the wand is designed for invoking and summoning.

In some traditions, there are only two ways to draw this pentagram. One is called an invoking pentagram and the other is called the banishing pentagram. I have used this system, and although it is effective, it lacks a great deal of power. In reality, there are actually ten ways to draw this pentagram: five invoking and five banishing. To invoke the power of a specific element, you should begin drawing the pentagram from the point that is represented by that element and go clockwise. To banish, draw from the point of the element and go counterclockwise.

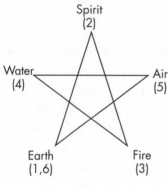

Invoking Earth Pentagram

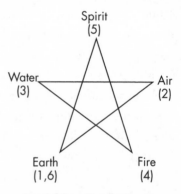

Banishing Earth Pentagram

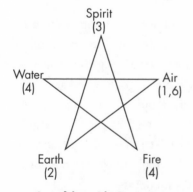

Invoking Air Pentagram

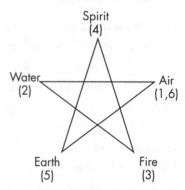

Banishing Air Pentagram

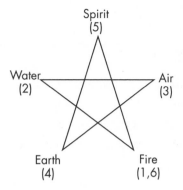

Invoking Fire Pentagram

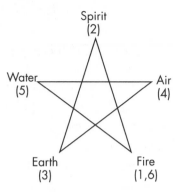

Banishing Fire Pentagram

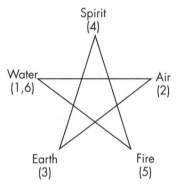

Invoking Water Pentagram

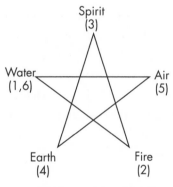

Banishing Water Pentagram

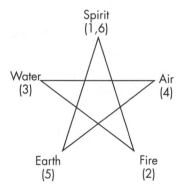

Invoking Spirit Pentagram

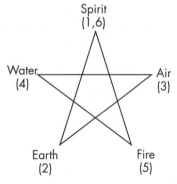

Banishing Spirit Pentagram

CONCERNING THE MAGICK CIRCLE

For the witch, everything on earth is sacred, and all places have a certain power that can be tapped into. This power is not always of a pure nature, however, and many times the area must be cleansed and purified before magical work can be performed there. This consecration of the ritual area is known as casting the magick circle.

In essence, the witch will etch a circle on the ground and then magically empower that circle to keep out all negative influences and energies and keep in all positive energies. This is done so that all the energy raised by the witch is contained within this magick circle until it is decided that enough energy has accumulated to accomplish the goal; then it is released.

Energy raising can be done in many different ways, which I have covered in detail in the chapter concerning this area. The circle is the temple of the witch, and because the circle can be cast, or erected, in any place and at any time, a witch can perform magick in any location without the need for a temple or church.

A Sample Circle Casting

Setting up the ritual area:

First you must clear out an area to act as the ritual area. If you are performing the ritual outdoors, as it should be, you must mark a circle on the ground. This can be done by taking a length of rope, tying the ends together, and laying it out in a circle. Many traditions instruct that the circle should be 9 feet in diameter. I personally find this a cramped space. When working alone I prefer a 13-foot diameter circle. This allows much more space for dancing and moving.

Use a small table to serve as your altar and place it in the north of the circle (see "Circle Setup," p. 67). In the center of the circle you

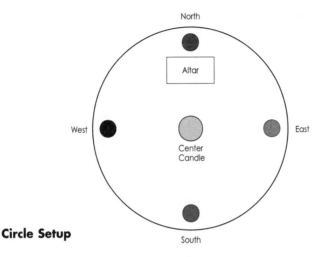

Circle Setup

should place a candle. Instead of a candle, I often use a can of Sterno. This is more practical when working outdoors because if there is a breeze the Sterno will remain lit, whereas a candle would go out. For quarter candles you should use the seven-day glass-encased candles; these will also remain lit outdoors better than regular tapered candles.

Place all of your witch tools onto the altar as shown in the diagram below.

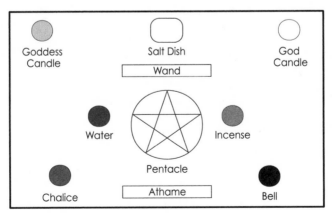

Altar Setup

Light all of the quarter candles. Take up your athame and move to the center of the circle and say:

> *Behold, for I a Priestless of the Old Ways do banish all illusion and phantoms.*

Move clockwise to the north and take up the dish of soil saying:

> *Now do I stoop down into a world of Darkness,*
> *the depths of which are unknown,*
> *and Hades casts a gloomy shroud;*
> *I open my spirit and hear the Voice of Earth.*

Draw an invoking pentagram of Earth and say:

> *In the names and powers of the Northern Quarter,*
> *I summon, stir, and call forth the spirits of the Earth.*

Feel the spirits of the element Earth rising up within you. Move to the east, place some incense on the charcoal and say:

> *Through the realm of Air come visions and voices,*
> *and my mind extends to greet them.*
> *Flashing, bounding, revolving, does the wind cry aloud;*
> *I open my spirit and I hear the Voice of Air.*

Draw an invoking pentagram of Air and say:

> *In the names of powers of the Eastern Quarter;*
> *I summon, stir and call forth the spirits of the Air.*

Feel the spirits of the element Air flowing around you. Move to the south, light the red candle and say:

> *I open my eyes and see before me a Holy and Formless Fire,*
> *A fire that lightens the hidden depths of the Universe.*

Banishing the shadows of illusion and darkness of night,
I open my spirit and I hear the Voice of Fire.

Trace an invoking pentagram of Fire and say:

In the names and powers of the Southern Quarter,
I summon, stir, and call forth the spirits of Fire.

Feel the spirits of the element Fire burning within you. Move to the west, take up the dish of water, sprinkle some onto the ground and say:

I, a Priest/ess of the Old Ways,
do Sprinkle with the Lustral Waters of the Sea,
and hear the sound of waves upon the shore;
I open my spirit and I hear the Voice of Water.

Feel the spirits of the element Water flowing through you. Trace an invoking pentagram of Water and say:

In the names and powers of the Western Quarter;
I summon, stir and call forth the spirits of Water.

Feel the spirits of the element Water flowing within you. Move to the center of the circle and stand facing the north. Above the center candle trace the invoking pentagram of Spirit. As you do so, say:

Earth, Air, Fire, and Water,
By the magick powers of witchcraft
and by this sacred sign (pentagram)
Do I invoke the Old Ones,
Guardians of these Sacred Rites.

Call to the god and goddess that you have chosen as your patrons and say the following:

I invoke you,
Lord and Lady of the celestial spheres.
You, whose dwelling place is in the invisible,
May your will be my will.
May my will be your will.
May we be as One
As was in days of Old.
The Will of the gods do I behold.

Now, for a few moments, stand and feel the power of the spirits and the god and goddess whom you have summoned forth. Hold this feeling for as long as you can. After a few moments, begin your ritual of magick or worship.

CHAPTER 6

THE WITCH'S TOOLS

*Through the charms of Thessalian witches . . .
they attract by the magic whirlings of the
twisted threads.*

—LUCAN, ROMAN POET

CONCERNING MAGICAL CORDS

The cord should be one of the first things a witch creates with his or her own hands. In the Church of Thessally, the first circle following the dedication of a new member is set aside for that dedicant to make the ritual cord. The cord is made from red yarn. Choose a bright, vibrant red rather than a maroon or burgundy red. Blood red is the best color to use, as it symbolizes the blood of life. The braiding of this cord is a bit tricky at first and may require the assistance of another person.

First, take the red yarn and pull three separate strands that are each three times your height. This can be done by standing on one end of the yarn and pulling it up to the crown of your head. Pinch the yarn where your first measure ends and place that part at the bottom of your feet and continue to pull the yarn until you reach your head again. Repeat one more time and you will have one strand of yarn that is three times your length. Cut the strand and lay it aside. Repeat this twice more, which will leave you with your three strands each three times your height.

Place the three strands together and stretch them out. As the yarn tends to tangle very easily, it helps if you have an assistant who can hold one end as you stretch the other end out. Once you have it stretched out and free of knots and tangles, fold it in half to find the middle.

Have your assistant hold all three strands together at this middle point. Now, from the center of the strands, where your assistant is holding them, you begin to braid outward to the left. Continue to braid until you have gone out about 1 inch from the center. Then return to the center and braid outward in the opposite direction until you have braided another inch. The result will be a braid about 2 inches long directly in the center of the length of yarn. Sound confusing? Well you haven't heard the half of it yet.

The next step is to fold the entire length of yarn in half. In other words, the part that you just braided will be folded in half, forming a loop. This will result in six strands of yarn that must be braided.

Pair the six strands off by twos—two to the left, two in the center, and two to the right—treating each pair of strands as one strand, and braid all the way down the remaining length, starting from the loop you just created. Continue to braid until the cord is the same length as you. When this is done, tie a knot in the end to hold the cord together and keep it from unraveling. Cut any excess yarn away, making certain to leave a short bundle of the yarn frayed at the end past the knot.

The end result should be a red braided cord that is the same length as you, with one end looped and the other end frayed. This is symbolic of the goddess (loop) and the god (frayed). They are on opposite ends, yet still part of the same cord. The symbolism of the cord goes very deep and should be the source of a meditation.

This cord can be used in a symbolic version of the Great Rite (see chapter 12) by placing the frayed end through the looped end. It can also be used for knot and cord magic and for bindings, or it may be worn about the waist or allowed to hang loosely over the shoulders as a stole. It is a sign of a witch and should be kept on or near your athame in a safe place. I keep my cord on my deity shrine when I am not using or wearing it.

The Witch's Ladder

The old grandmother who made it wove and knotted into the witches' ladder every kind of ache and pain she could think of.

—ANONYMOUS AUTHOR

This bit of cord magick is an old spell that has been practiced for centuries and is sometimes called the "witch's garland." The witch's ladder was traditionally used to curse an enemy, but I have used it for beneficial purposes with great results.

To perform it you will first gather together items that represent your goal, or the outcome you want the spell to have. You should use an odd number of items, as even numbers are deemed magically unlucky. Three, seven, nine, and thirteen items are the most effective and most common numbers used.

These symbolic items must be objects small enough to be tied up and held with a knot. Feathers of a color sympathetic to the goal (see the appendix) are what I mostly use. These feathers in combination with petitions and symbols drawn on pieces of paper and rolled up like scrolls work extremely well. Remember, these items do not all have to be different. Three of the same colored feathers or nine scrolls with the same petition or symbols on them is fine.

Once you have your items assembled and your black/white cord at hand, take a few minutes to calm your mind and focus on your goal. Bring your attention to your need and concentrate on nothing else.

Take up your first item and tie a knot around it while focusing on your need or desire. Take up the second item and do the same. Repeat this action, each time focusing harder and harder on your desire. A simple chant can be used with each knot to help focus your mind on the task you are working on (see Concerning Chants, chapter 4). Once you have tied all of the knots, your ladder is complete.

Now comes the most important part of the spell. In succession, from the first item to the last, blow with three short breaths upon the knots that tie the symbols. This is the act of "breathing life" into the spell and activates the power of the ladder. Once you have blown on all of the knots, the ladder is empowered and should be hung in a corner of your home.

A good ladder to hang is one to keep negativity out of the home. Use your black/white cord for this one and tie four black feathers and three white feathers into it. Hang this ladder in your attic or in the west corner of your home.

A Binding Spell

For this spell, you will need to use your black cord. It is designed to bind or halt the actions of another person against harming you or others.

To perform this spell, you will need a wax image of the person you wish to bind. The color of the wax is not very important. For bindings, many witches choose black wax; some would rather use the natural color of the wax, which is actually a very light tan. Some witches prefer to mold the figures themselves out of beeswax. I have no skill whatsoever in sculpting, so I usually buy figure candles for this type of work, and I find they work just as well; they are available in a wide variety of colors.

Once you have the wax image of the person, you must carve the person's name in the bottom of the figure and verbally "name" the candle aloud. To do this you simply point to the candle and say: "No longer are you just a waxen image, but now I give you life and your name shall be _____."

Visualize the wax figure as the person whom you wish to bind. It helps the spell if you have a tag-lock of the person. A tag-lock can be a photograph (Polaroids are best), a piece of hair or fingernail, some article of clothing, blood, or even urine. I have once performed an effective binding spell on an individual who threatened to curse a friend of mine by using the dust from within his footprint as he walked through the college campus. The tag-lock is your link to that person and makes the spell much easier and infinitely more effective.

If you have a tag-lock, before you name the image you should place the tag-lock in the heart region of the image. To do this you heat up a large needle and stick it into the heart area of the wax doll. Wiggle the needle around to make the hole a little larger. Take your tag-lock and place it into this hole. If the tag-lock is a photograph, then you burn it and place the ashes into the hole. Now, drip some more wax, of the same color, over the hole to seal it up.

Once you have the tag-lock in place and the image named, begin to wrap the image up in your black cord. This should be done on the night of the new moon. Start at the feet of the image and begin wrapping the image in a counterclockwise direction. As you wrap, repeat the following chant:

(Person's name) *with ropes of black I wrap and bind,*
To stop your evil and confuse your mind.
No longer can you cause harm to anyone or me;
This I will, and so shall it be.

Repeat this chant three times while wrapping the image completely around from bottom to top. Tie off the remaining cord so that it does not unravel and hang the image in a dark place in your home. Keep it there for one full moon cycle and the spell is done.

This spell works by magically tying up the person causing harm. In a sense, you have the offender bound and gagged in the corner. When you feel that the person can no longer cause any harm, you can take the image down and untie it. To reverse the spell, you chant the following three times as you unravel the image.

By my magick have you been bound,
Sending your evil into the ground.
Now that you are no threat to anyone or me;
By my magick, I set you free.

The cord should be ritually cleansed by soaking it in the green blood mixture for purification (see Concerning the Green Blood, chapter 8). Let the cord soak for one day and then hand wash it and let it hang dry in the sun. After this it can be reused. If you feel that the person would only do more harm once the spell is released, you should bury the image in the ground, preferably near a crossroads, and braid yourself a new cord.

Cord Spell for Healing

For this spell you will need your red cord and a healing green blood mixture (see Concerning the Green Blood, chapter 8). This spell works best if the person who needs the healing is physically present. If, however, the person is bedridden or in a hospital, you can use a figure candle with a tag-lock, "naming" it just as you did in the above ritual; only in this case it will be used to heal the person. The process is the same whether the person is present or not, so I will assume that the person is present in this description.

Seat the person down in the center of the room or place the image of the person in the center of your altar. Make certain that he or she is comfortable. Allow the person a few moments to get situated and relaxed. Playing some soft music helps to set the quiet mood. I use a recording of the sound of wind blowing through the trees. You may also want to offer a cup of chamomile tea about fifteen minutes prior to the healing to aid in relaxing the client.

Once the person is relaxed, you will begin the spell. Rub your hands together vigorously until they are very hot. This magnetizes the hands and allows them to draw off any negative energy. Take your cord and soak it in the healing green blood, which you should have prepared earlier. If you like, and I find that this helps the healing process, let the client see you make the green blood. When your magnetized hands touch the cord and the green blood they will "stimulate" the powers of these things, adding more of your power to the powers of the mixture and the spell.

Now take the cord out of the green blood and wring out any excess liquid. Hold the cord tightly, about one foot across, letting the ends hang down, and begin sweeping it back and forth over the client's head, never actually touching the client. For example: Stand behind the client, who is seated in front of you; hold the cord tightly at a length of about one foot across. Reach over the client's head and lower the cord to neck level; come back up and over the front of the client's face, over the top of the head, and then down behind the neck. Do this three times very quickly.

While doing this you must visualize that you are sweeping away the sickness in their bodies. Now move clockwise and stand at the left side of the client and perform the same sweeping action, only this time you will sweep from the right shoulder, over the head and to the left shoulder. Do this three times as well. Now move clockwise again and stand in front of the client. Sweep with the cord from the back of the head, over the top, and down in front of the face. Finally, move to the client's right hand side and sweep from the left shoulder, over the head and down to the right shoulder. All the sweeping motions should be done in multiples of three. This will result in twelve sweeps of the head area.

Now place the cord back into the green blood mixture to "remove the ill energy" that it has absorbed. Take it out once again and wring out the excess liquid. Have your client stand up and begin sweeping the entire body. Start from behind the client. Sweep from the top of the head, down the back to the floor. Repeat three times. Move to the client's left and sweep that side of the body three times, then to the front of the client and eventually to the right side of the client. Once this is done, soak the cord again in the green blood to remove ill energy and wring it out. Tie the cord around the client's waist and tell him or her to wear it the entire day, even while sleeping. In the morning, the client is to go out and bury the cord, and health will follow quickly. As the cord deteriorates in the earth, so does the illness wither away to nothing.

I have used this healing technique with great success and have cured afflictions that modern medical practices were unable to cure. Remember, however, that you should always make certain that your client has consulted a physician about their illness. This is especially true for serious illnesses. Magick works when performed correctly and with enthusiasm, but sometimes if a situation must be, no amount of magick can reverse it, just as there are times when no amount of medical attention will effect a cure.

A Charm to Ward off the Evil Eye

This spell utilizes cord magic to overcome the "evil eye." The belief that one can be cursed with a glance exists in nearly every culture in the world and therefore has literally countless charms to protect against it. The evil eye is a real threat, and it does not take a "trained" person to cause harm with a glance. The eyes are powerful projectors of energy, and if someone looks to you with evil intentions or even a high degree of jealousy or spite, that energy may hook into your aura and stay there, thus bringing about a run of "bad luck." To prevent this from happening or to negate the effects of it if it has happened already, perform the ritual below.

ITEMS NEEDED

- Cord braided of black and red yarn
- Hex-breaking green blood

Before beginning this ritual, take a spiritual bath. Pour one 12-ounce bottle of beer into the bath. I know this may sound strange or humorous, but the hops and barley used to make beer act as a wonderful cleansing agent against the energies associated with the evil eye. (See chapter 7 for various spiritual baths.)

Braid the cord as I explained in the beginning of the chapter. As you braid, chant the following:

> *Braided to measure, wrought to bind,*
> *Negativity I leave behind.*
> *I bind it up into this twine;*
> *Peace and Serenity now be mine.*

Braid the cord until it is your height and then place it into the hex-breaking green blood mixture and let it soak as you say:

> *By the Power of this Green Blood mix,*
> *The power of this charm I fix.*
> *To keep all negativity bound away,*
> *Keep it far from me both night and day.*

Repeat this chant three times as you project your energy into the mixture. Take the cord out of the green blood and hang it in the sun to dry. The energy of the sun will also infuse the cord with protective powers.

Once the cord is dried, tie seven knots in it to bind any harm coming to you. Carry this cord with you, and all negativity will be captured in the knots and kept safely away from your aura. This type of charm should only be worn for one moon cycle and then discarded. A new one is then made and worn again. Continue this until you feel that there is no longer a threat of the evil eye.

CONCERNING THE ATHAME

The athame, or witch's knife, is used during rituals. The athame is a knife with a double-edged blade and a black handle. The symbolism of the athame connects it to the Moon, the silver blade representing the full moon and the black handle representing the new moon. It is also the representation of the male phallus and thus the masculine aspect of nature. Some traditions attribute the athame to the element air, but I have found this to be confusing. The athame is made of steel, and therefore it must be forged. During the forging process, the metal will accumulate huge amounts of fire energy, and so I attribute the athame to that element. This works quite well, and I encourage you to try it.

When casting a circle, it is the athame that you use to project the energy. Visualize the energy issuing from the tip of the blade like a laser. The athame also acts as a magical weapon against negative energies and spirits by cutting through their deception. However, never physically cut anything with your athame and do not allow any other person to touch it once it is consecrated. If someone should happen to touch it, simply wash it down with water and ammonia (just a drop of ammonia) and reconsecrate it.

Concerning the Magical Wand

In *Witchcraft Today* by Dr. Gerald Gardner, the good doctor says that the wand was not a part of traditional European witchcraft but was something that was borrowed from ceremonial magicians by the witch cult and adapted to their use. For this reason, many covens do not place much emphasis on wands or even use one at all but rather use the athame for all things. While this is effective, it also leaves out a wide variety of opportunities. Wands are most often used when working and dealing with invocational rites and rituals. While the athame, or any tool for that matter, is also effective for this, the wand adds a special touch. It is my personal practice to have one wand for general purposes and several other "special-purpose" wands.

A wand should be made by hand and can be as elaborate as the witch wants it to be. However, there are some guidelines that should be followed when constructing your wand.

1. Your wand should be one cubit in length. A cubit is the distance from your elbow to the tip of your middle finger.
2. The wand should be hollowed out and filled with appropriate herbs, oils, or condensers that are in accordance with the purpose the wand will serve.

3. The wand should either be capped at both ends, or capped at one end with a crystal at the top.

4. When using a crystal at the top of the wand, the point of the crystal should be clear and unchipped.

The material to use for constructing a wand is left entirely up to the witch; however, I find that the best magical wands are constructed of elder wood. The elder tree has a long magical history and has been associated with witchcraft, fairy lore, and magick since as far back as history can record. Elder wood makes a wonderful wand because the branches grow relatively straight and the center is filled with a soft pith that is easily removed, leaving the center hollow.

Rite of the Wand

Here is the ritual I used to prepare my magical wand. The first part of this process starts nine days before the full moon. Before sunrise, go to the tree you have chosen to cut from and pour an offering of apricot nectar to the spirit of the elder tree. When cutting from and elder tree, it is also important that you not only leave an offering to the tree's numen (spirit), but also to the goddess known as Lady Ellhorne, who is the protectress of these sacred trees. After pouring your libation (sacred offering of fluid) to the tree spirit, leave a plate of bread and a glass of wine to Lady Ellhorne and say the following prayer:

> *Lady Ellhorne, Guardian of the sacred Elder Trees.*
> *I pray to you on bended knees.*
> *A branch from this tree I wish to take.*
> *From it, a magick wand to make.*
> *As a follower of the Old Ways I ask;*
> *Lend thy power unto my task.*

By the Earth, the Moon and Sun.
In the name of magick be it done.

At this point, draw a circle around the tree and take three sticks of incense (frankincense is best) and place them in the ground around the tree, two to the back and one to the front where you are sitting. Light them and sit quietly meditating on the power of the elder tree and the wand you wish to fashion.

Look at the tree and locate the branch for your wand. When the incense sticks have burned out, take out your saw or machete, tap the branch you want three times, and quickly cut it off. Wrap the branch in a white cloth and take it home. Remove the bark and, using a coat hanger, dig the pith out of the center. Let the branch dry for three days.

Sand the branch smooth and cut it to the required length of one cubit. Cap one end of the wand with a copper cap, which can be purchased in the plumbing section of any hardware store. When you have the end capped off, you need to find a small clear-tipped quartz crystal to place at the other end. Before placing the crystal into the wand permanently, you must first fill the wand with appropriate condensers.

Melt some white wax in a double boiler. Add three pinches of the herbs rue, fennel, and vervain (all herbs sacred to witchcraft) to the melted wax and then pour the wax into the center of the wand until it is full. Place the crystal in the end of the wand and wrap some leather cord around the base of the crystal to hold it on the wand. You can use hot glue to seal the crystal and fix it in place.

On the night of the full moon, at midnight, go outside with your wand and hold it up to the moon and say:

My Lady, Mistress of Magick and pale Moonlight;
You who rules the star-filled heavens of Night.
Bless and empower this wand of magick
That all may see, and know thy greatness.

Wherefore do I consecrate and dedicate this wand
To you, Great Mistress of Magick.

With that done, take the wand inside and paint the symbols of magick on it. I generally paint the wand yellow and then paint the symbols of the planets.

CONCERNING THE CHALICE AND THE PENTACLE

The chalice serves the purpose of holding the sacred wine or ale that is used in rituals. It is the representation of the element of water and also symbolizes the womb of the goddess. After completing a ceremony where power is raised, you should always sit and eat some bread and drink some wine or ale. The act of eating and drinking grounds the energies within you and is a sign that the rite is complete. The chalice is usually made of glass or silver and requires no special preparation other than a simple cleansing and charging; then it is presented to the gods and devoted to their service.

The pentacle is the tool that represents the element earth, and it is simply a small wooden or clay disk with the symbol of the pentagram painted upon it. Different traditions vary as to what symbols should be on the pentacle, but if you are practicing alone, a simple pentagram will suffice. The pentacle should be placed directly in the center of the altar as the foundation of your practices. In the Church of Thessally, when initiates move up through the degree advancements, they are made to swear their oaths with one hand upon the pentacle.

CONCERNING THE BOOK OF SHADOWS

According to tradition, all witches keep a magical spell book called the Book of Shadows. Although various explanations exist as to how this custom came into being, it is my opinion that the Book of Shadows was not part of early witchcraft, as the people practicing witchcraft were, for the most part, illiterate and learned their craft from family traditions passed down by word of mouth. As cities grew larger and the country people were introduced to reading and writing, knowledge was exchanged between the traditional witches who practiced folk magic and the ceremonial magicians who practiced in the temples of the cities. I believe the Book of Shadows is something that witchcraft borrowed from ceremonial magick.

Regardless of where the idea came from, keeping a list of your potions, recipes, spells, rituals, and dreams is a very good idea. Nobody can be expected to memorize every single spell or attribute by heart. Over time you will, through practice, learn the most common rituals and spells. The more obscure and least used spells should be written down for later use.

Today you can choose from a wide selection of blank books that can be used as a Book of Shadows. There are even some books available with "Book of Shadows" embossed on the cover. In earlier times, the most common color for the cover was green. Today, however, the most common color seems to be black.

There are certain rules regarding the Book of Shadows that should be adhered to:

1. All information should be handwritten. This is sometimes done in a secret code known only to the witch who wrote it. This is a safety precaution so that anyone finding the book will not know what it says. During the witch-burning times this was said to protect the witch so that no specific handwriting could be attributed to the book, nor could it be understood. In today's society this is not so much a problem anymore. However, I have seen new students try to steal their priest or priestess's Book of Shadows in order to get spells or

recipes to use for their own ends. It is my custom to write all group rituals, or any information that is available to anyone who researches, in standard English. But, I write all of my personal spells and rituals in code.

2. The color of the ink used to write in your Book of Shadows is not important, but the most common that I have seen is blue. I believe this is a practical application, as blue ink shows up easier in candlelight than does black or other colors.

3. The first page of the Book of Shadows should contain a magical sigil of power. Again, the most common being the upright pentagram.

4. Never loan your Book of Shadows to another person. Should someone wish to copy something from your book, and you consent, let the person copy it while in your sight. If you let the book leave your sight, you may never see it again. It has happened before.

5. Be creative with your book. Draw pictures, write poetry, songs, whatever comes to your mind and speaks to your spirit.

6. It is not necessary to consecrate your Book of Shadows prior to using it, although I would recommend that you do so. By consecration, you astrally cleanse the book from any previous energy it may have picked up, and you also set it apart from an ordinary book.

Consecration of the Book of Shadows

This is a rather long and complicated ritual for the consecration of the Book of Shadows, but it is very effective. It charges the book with an aura of mystery that can be felt by any who look upon the book.

Set up your ritual area, and the altar should have a white altar cloth. Place the book on the altar opened to the first page, where your sigil of power is. Light both your god and goddess candles and kneel before the altar. Recite the following:

God and Goddess, Lord and Lady, Father and Mother of all Life, think, even for a moment, upon this, thy worshipper who kneels before you. I call upon thee and invoke thee to attend and witness this ritual performed in thy honor and thy craft.

Move to the Northern Quarter:

Spirits and Powers of the Fertile Earth, I summon, stir, and call thee forth. Attend this ritual of consecration and lend thy powers unto my purpose.

Move to the Eastern Quarter:

Spirits and Powers of the Rushing Wind, I summon, stir, and call thee forth. Attend this ritual of consecration and lend thy powers unto my purpose.

Move to the Southern Quarter:

Spirits and Powers of the Flame, I summon, stir and call thee forth. Attend this ritual of consecration and lend thy powers unto my purpose.

Move to the Western Quarter:

Spirits and Powers of the Resounding Sea, I summon, stir, and call thee forth. Attend this ritual of consecration and lend thy powers unto my purpose.

Now you will call in the Watchers to attend and witness the rite. Go again to the North and hold your hands above your head and say:

Great Watcher of the Northern Quarter, by the Mighty Star Fomalhaut do I summon thee to attend and witness this ritual. Guard my Sacred Circle that I may perform in comfort and solitude these ancient rites.

Go to the East and raise your hands high and say:

Great Watcher of the Eastern Quarter, by the Mighty Star Aldeboran do I summon thee to attend and witness this ritual. Guard my Sacred Circle that I may perform in comfort and solitude these ancient rites.

Go to the South and raise your hands high and say:

Great Watcher of the Southern Quarter, by the Mighty Star Regulus do I summon thee to attend and witness this ritual. Guard my Sacred Circle that I may perform in comfort and solitude these ancient rites.

Go to the West and raise your hands high and say:

Great Watcher of the Western Quarter, by the Mighty Star Antares do I summon thee to attend and witness this ritual. Guard my Sacred Circle that I may perform in comfort and solitude these ancient rites.

Sit in the center of the circle and feel the powers of the god and goddess and the elemental spirits around you. After a few moments, stand up and state the purpose of your rite.

I, (state your name) *do perform this rite of consecration, in the witness and with the aid of the Great Mother and Father God and all ye spirits of nature. Receive this book of magick as the storehouse of thy powers and let all that be written herein be a direct expression of thy divine and spiritual will.*

With this done, trace over the sigil of power with anointing oil, using the index finger of your dominant hand. Close the book and anoint the four corners of the book with anointing oil.

Afterwards, incense the book with an incense of the planetary power for that day. This ritual should be repeated for seven days. Each day fumigate the book with the appropriate incense of the planet ruling that day.

Sunday - benzoin
Monday - myrrh
Tuesday - dragon's blood
Wednesday - cinquefoil (five-finger grass)
Thursday - hyssop
Friday - vervain
Saturday - patchouli

After the seven days, wrap the book in white linen and put it in a secret place for one moon cycle. After that time period, you can remove the book and use it as needed. Every full moon you should fumigate it with the appropriate planetary incense and anoint the sigil and four corners with anointing oil. By reanointing on the full of the moon, you link the book to the moon cycles, and thus it begins to store lunar energy. Never let the book see the light of the sun. Keep it locked away in a safe place.

CONCERNING THE WITCH'S BOTTLE

The witch's bottle is a weapon of defense used by a witch as protection against another witch's or magician's magick. There are many different ways to make witch's bottles, and no one really knows from where the concept of the bottle originated.

In the 1950s several large bottles were unearthed from beneath the foundations of some old houses in England. These bottles had a thin neck and a large body with the face of a bearded man embossed on them. The face was attributed to that of Cardinal Bellarmine, and thus the bottles were called "Bellarmine jugs." However, when the jugs were unstopped the contents of the bottles were rather noxious— human hair, fingernail clippings, nails, broken glass or needles, salt, and urine. These items baffled many of the people who uncovered the bottles, but to those schooled in witchcraft, it was recognized as a very old practice of magical protection. In fact, the face that was attributed to Cardinal Bellarmine is actually a depiction of the ancient Celtic god Cernunnos. In earlier examples of this bottle, the face is not one face but three faces combined as one, which was how the god Cernunnos was often shown. Over the years, the face was simplified into one powerful-looking countenance.

Instructions for Making a Witch's Bottle

ITEMS NEEDED

- An empty and cleaned out mayonnaise jar (6 oz.)
- A red cloth cut into the shape of a heart
- Some of your own hair clippings
- Some of your own nail clippings
- 13 iron nails
- 13 black-headed pins
- 1 cup of sea salt

The making of a witch's bottle is very simple and should be done as early on in your practices as you possibly can. Next to the athame, I consider the witch's bottle one of the most important items to be made. Never let another person know that you are making the bottle, or the reason for doing so.

The Witch's Tools

1. Place all of the items on your altar and take a few moments to meditate on the task at hand. You are performing a rite of protection for your magical safety.
2. Take up the hair and the nail clippings and place them into the jar saying:

    Here do I present myself.

3. Take up the thirteen iron nails and place them into the jar saying:

    Here are my swords of protection

4. Take up the salt and place it into the jar saying:

    Here is salt to purify me and keep me clean and safe.

5. Take up the red heart-shaped cloth. Hold it high and say:

    Here is the heart of any who wish me harm.

6. Stick all thirteen black-headed pins into the cloth heart and say:

    *Let any who wish me harm or any who wish me ill
    Feel the pain of their own heart's hate, rebounded by this
    witch's Will.*

7. Place the pin-studded heart into the jar.
8. Next, fill the jar with your own urine. I know this sounds rather disgusting, but urine is a very powerful fluid condenser. If you look to your own primal instincts, urinating on something is symbolic of saying how worthless you think it is. This is in effect what you are doing. You are stating, symbolically, that you know any spell that is cast against you is a useless and worthless gesture, and this is the frame of mind you should take while performing this act.

9. When the jar is filled, or at least halfway so, screw the cap on and paint a protective pentagram in red on the top of the lid. Take the jar out on the night of the new moon and bury it somewhere near your home. As you are burying the jar, say the following:

    Blessed Mother of the Darkened Moon
    I pray that you grant me this boon.
    A bottle of protection do I bury here,
    To protect me from those both far and near.
    May any curse or magick spell
    Placed on me be dispelled.
    Rebounded on the sender be.
    In accordance with the Law of Three.

10. Now cover the jar with dirt and seal the dig by tracing an upright triangle in the soil. Stand up, turn, and walk away without looking back. Once the bottle is buried, it should never be dug up again. To do so would be to release all of the negativity that it has absorbed for you. If another person digs up the bottle, it will have no effect, as the bottle is designed to absorb negativity aimed directly to you. This energy is tied to you and you alone, and cannot affect another person.

I have often been asked whether one should dig up the witch's bottle, when moving from the home where it is buried, and rebury it at the new home. The answer to this is a resounding *No!* Do not dig up the bottle for any reason. If you move to a new location, the bottle will continue to work for you. However, it is a good idea to make another bottle and bury it at the new location. One can never have too many protective devices.

There are those who say that a witch's bottle will have reached its capacity after several years, and then a new one must be made. I have found this to be erroneous. The witch's bottle is buried in the earth so that the earth may ground the energies of the negativity directed toward you. One bottle should be all that is needed.

If you feel that at some point in time you are under the attack of another, it could be that your witch's bottle has broken. In this case it would be necessary to make another. Also, there will be times when your witch's bottle may not offer complete protection. This could be for various reasons. Perhaps the person spelling against you is stronger than your protection. We all know that a steel sword will slice through a bronze shield. Another way that this can happen is if the person has a *tag-lock* on you. A tag-lock is a personal item such as clothing, a photo, a lock of hair, a fingernail, anything that is directly associated to you. Through an item such as this, another may sidestep your protection, and their magick can affect you. Also, a person can place magically charged items into a food dish or a drink and present it to you. If you ingest this item, then the spell has taken effect and circumvented all of your protections. If this happens to you, you would need to consult the coin oracle for guidance on removing this condition. (See Witch's Coin Divination, chapter 10). These things may seem to be a bit on the paranoid side, but I assure you they do happen. Witches must be knowledgeable in all forms of magick in order to assure their safety and the safety of those they love or work for.

CONCERNING CANDLES

The most popular and common form of magical spells is performed using candles. The use of candles stems as far back as ancient Egypt where oil lamps were used in the casting of spells and in religious rites. The magick of the candle lies in its ability to shine light where once there was only darkness. These days, candles can be purchased in nearly any color and in a wide variety of shapes and sizes. These all are wonderful for magick, but always remember that the power of the spell is within you, the witch, and not the special type of candle. So if the spell calls for a blue seven-knobbed candle remember that you could substitute it with a regular blue candle or even a white candle. I have, on occasion, worked effective candle spells using tiny birthday candles when nothing else was available.

When working with candle magick, Fire is the activating element of the spell. When dealing with fire, spells will manifest quickly and sometimes harshly. Remember, Fire warms, but it also burns. Be careful how you use the powers of witchcraft, remember the Law of Return.

Many books give very complex rituals involving up to a dozen candles, and these are very effective, but also difficult to perform correctly. This is especially true when you are performing magick for others. I can fit a dozen candles on my altar, but I often perform rituals for dozens of people a week, and it would be difficult to work these spells for everyone, simply because I only have so much space. In my experience, I have found that one or two candles are more than enough to work most spells effectively.

TYPES OF CANDLES AND THEIR USES:

- *Tapered Candles* - These are the standard household stick candles that come in every conceivable color. They are excellent for candle magick; however, you must never leave them burning unattended, and they also require a fireproof candleholder.

- *Seven-Day Candles* - These are very common in South Louisiana where they are commonly called novena candles or prayer candles. These candles stand roughly nine inches tall and are encased in glass. I find myself using these candles the most, as they can be left unattended without worrying about a fire breaking out. These candles come in an enormous variety of colors and even in combinations of different colors.

- *Black Cat Candles* - These candles come only in black and are shaped like a cat. They are used primarily for hex-breaking spells.
- *Skull Candles* - These candles come in both black and red and are used to break curses and sometimes to place curses on others.
- *Mummy Candles* - These candles resemble an Egyptian sarcophagus or an actual mummy. They are used mostly to break curses and sometimes to help draw money to you.

Candle Spell for Money

ITEMS NEEDED:

- Brown seven-day candle (for fast money)
- Dollar bill
- Silver coin
- Ground cinnamon (to bring money)

This spell is short, sweet, and effective. Take the brown candle and sprinkle a pinch of cinnamon on the top of the candle. Now wrap the silver coin up in the dollar bill and place them both beneath the candle. As you light the candle say the following chant:

> *By candle light and magick flame,*
> *By this magick in the Old One's name,*
> *Money I do draw to me.*
> *As I will, so shall it be.*

Let the candle burn until it is completely out. Each day you should go before the candle and repeat the chant again while you focus on the needed money. By the time the candle goes out or shortly thereafter you will have your money.

A Candle Spell to Break a Curse
ITEMS NEEDED:

- Black seven-day candle
- White seven-day candle
- Slice of lemon
- Small circular mirror (like from a makeup compact)
- Salt

This spell is one of the most effective spells to remove unwanted influences in our lives. This spell works by sending back any negative energy sent to us by others. Clear off your altar and place the black candle to the left side and the white candle to the right side. Now between the candles lay the mirror with the reflective side up. On the mirror place the slice of lemon and then sprinkle a little salt on top of the lemon.

Light the black candle and say:

> *Black candle burn away this hate;*
> *To fail is not within my fate;*
> *Someone wishes to bring me shame;*
> *Send it back from whence it came.*

Light the white candle and say:

> *White candle burn to bring in the light.*
> *By this spell do I set things right;*

No longer am I crossed or doomed;
My normal life is now resumed.

Repeat this chant each day over the candles until they are completely burned out. When the spell is complete, check the lemon. If there is some mold on the lemon, it means that the spell must be repeated. There is still more negative energy coming to you. Consult the coin oracle (see Witch's Coin Divination, chapter 10) to see if there is any other reason for your misfortune. If the lemon has dried up without molding, it means that the spell was successful and you no longer are the victim of psychic attack.

CONCERNING THE USE OF STATUES FOR WORSHIP

In ancient times, people traveled for many miles to make the pilgrimage to a temple; there they would leave offerings at the foot of a statue of the deity to whom the temple belonged. This was done in the hope that the deity would then look with favor upon the individual and grant blessings.

With the coming of Christianity the practice of praying at the foot of statues was shunned (the only exception being the Roman Catholic Church). The bible speaks of Moses becoming angry when he returned from the Mount with the Ten Commandments and saw the people worshipping the image of a golden bull. In disgust, Moses smashed the tablets containing the Ten Commandments. This attitude was taken up by many fervent Christians and pagans in the early days of Christianity. They ransacked each other's temples and smashed the statues of the deities. By doing so, many of them believed that they were in essence destroying the deity and proving the superiority of their god over the others' gods.

Even today in the magical community, there are those who feel that the use of statues in worship is a foolish practice. Those who feel this way simply do not understand what the use of statues in worship truly means.

First, notice that I say "use of statues in worship" and not "the worship of statues." There is a profound difference between the two. Indeed, it would be foolish to kneel before a statue and pray to it, believing the statue to actually be the deity. That is not what statues are for. A statue of a deity is a link to that particular deity. When I kneel or pray before my deity shrine, I have a variety of statues present. These statues are there to remind me of my various gods and goddesses and to provide them a comfortable atmosphere in which they can descend and hear my prayers.

Those who practice ceremonial magick will quickly admit that when performing any type of invocational or evocational rite, the magician must use the correct lighting, sigil, incense, oils, candles, colors, and other items associated with the spirit being contacted. This is done because the spirit will more easily come if the items that it likes or exists in or rules over are present. The same is true for statues. Deities will descend and attend rituals more easily if they have their representation present within the circle.

Also, when leaving offerings to the deity at the foot of a statue, you must pray earnestly, asking the deity to descend and accept the offering. The most common offerings being plants, special drinks such as Ambrosia, or various food items. Once the offering has dried up or evaporated, it is considered accepted by the deity and can be removed. If the item (particularly a food item) begins to mold or rot, it is a sign that the deity has not accepted the offering. Divination will answer why the offering was refused.

Statues can also be used as storehouses for energy. This is done by calling down the deity that the statue represents into the statue itself.

This allows the statue to absorb the energy of the deity. This energy can then be drawn upon in times of need. In ancient times there were many statues of various deities that were attributed with incredible powers. For example, there was a statue of Mercury in the center of the town Achaia in Pharis. People would first burn frankincense and light candles before the statue. Then they would place a coin in the right hand of the statue (as an offering) and whisper their question in the right ear of the statue. After this was done, they would stop up their ears and walk away, not looking back. Once out of the square, they would unstop their ears and the first phrase or voice they heard was the prophecy or guidance they needed. This message was considered to be directly inspired by Mercury himself.

Also in Achaia, in a town called Bura there was a temple to Hercules where one would pray before a statue of the god and then toss a die onto an oracular board. Depending on how the die fell, the board offered a certain interpretation of the question asked.

In *The Gospel of Aradia* there is a story about three children whose family had no food to eat. One day when picking flowers in a garden, they happened upon a statue of the goddess Diana. The young girl in the group placed flowers at the foot of the statue and crowned the goddess's image with flowers. The magician Virgil happened along and told the children how to pray for the goddess's descent into the statue. Upon doing so the children left the garden. The next morning they found a freshly killed deer at the foot of the statue, which fed the family for many days.

The process of making a statue into a storehouse of power is a long process that requires much research and intuition. You must research the deity to find out what animals, plants, days, metal, stones, and so on are attributed to the deity. All of these must be combined together to make a suitable link. If you are sculpting the statue yourself, you can place some of these items in the clay before you sculpt, thus incorporating the items directly into the statue. If you are like me, and not at all artistically inclined, you can purchase a statue and use it just the same, with the same results.

Ritual for Empowering a Statue

This is a ritual that I used to empower a statue of Hekate, my patron. This statue has affected many people who have come into contact with it in wonderful ways. During this same ritual, as I charged the statue, I was in the company of an author who was a so-called "authority" on the craft. During the ritual we were kneeling before the altar, and when we looked up, the statue of Hekate seemed to shimmer and shake. Then, suddenly, she began to dance. I know this sounds impossible, but it is absolutely the truth. Other people, upon praying to Hekate before the statue, have also seen it begin to dance. The following ritual is to give you an example; it can be used, with a few changes, to empower the statue or object of any deity.

ITEMS NEEDED

- A statue of the deity (in this example, Hekate)
- Hekate blend incense
- 1 self–igniting charcoal
- 3 white mice (sacred to Hekate)
- Wormwood (sacred to Hekate)
- A wooden box in which to place the statue when not in use
- White paint and a small paintbrush
- Ornaments or offerings to be placed with the statue

This ritual is an adaptation of that given in the *Chaldean Oracles* which say that Hekate herself speaks of how her statues should be pre-

pared for use. Once again, to adapt this ritual to any other deity simply replace these items with items sacred to that deity and reword the
ritual appropriately.

1. Place the deity statue standing up on the center of your altar.
   Place the box that will house the statue when not in use lying
   horizontally at the feet of the statue.

2. Sprinkle wormwood (or other sacred herb) in a circle around
   the box and statue. Now take some white paint and paint
   three white mice on the bottom or back of the statue—one
   mouse for each face of the goddess. When performing this
   rite for another deity, use symbols and herbs appropriate to
   that god or goddess. Research is the key to determining these
   symbols.

3. Place your offerings in the box. With the goddess Hekate do
   not be cheap. She enjoys rich adornments. Remember, these
   are offerings to the goddess, not a priest or priestess. In my
   box, I placed pearls, onyx, and sapphires, which are sacred to
   Hekate.

4. Take your charcoal and place it in a fireproof container filled
   with sand. Next, sprinkle some of your incense on the charcoal and incense the entire statue and box. For Hekate, the
   box should be made from the wood of a bay tree, but pine
   works quite well, not just for Hekate, but for all deities. Pine
   also has the quality of acting as a barrier against astral energy
   and spirits. Thus it keeps the contents within the box safe
   from negativity that might be projected by others and also
   keeps the energy of the statue safely contained within, so as
   not to attract unnecessary spirits to it. Coffins were originally
   made of pine because of this barrier effect; it kept the spirit of
   the person from coming out and haunting the living.

5.   Now say the following words:

> *Hekate, Goddess of the Crossroads and Wanderer of the Dark Heavens.*
> *Descend, I pray thee, and take residence for a moment within this, thy image.*
> *For I have performed the rite, which thou hast thyself commanded.*
> *Fulfill thy promise and speak to me of things most secret.*
> *Reveal unto me the mysteries which I seek to solve.*

> *Hekate, Goddess of the Night,*
> *Descend and appear unto my sight.*

   (Repeat this chant three times)

6.   Now place the three white mice on the altar as an offering to the goddess. Let them run about for a while and observe their behavior. The mice will be the key to let you know if the goddess has answered. If they begin to congregate about the statue or box, Hekate has descended. If they scatter off and try to escape, she has not descended, and you must repeat the invocation until she arrives. This may take some time; however, it has been my experience with Hekate that she descends readily. Be prepared for an intense energy increase.

   Keep in mind that Hekate may not manifest into physical appearance, although she has been known to do so, as I can testify. However, more often she will speak through your dreams.

7.   When the rite is done, dismiss the goddess with a thank-you and either release the mice to the wild or keep them as pets.

8. Place the statue in the box with the offerings and keep it out of sight. Each night, you should take the statue out, give an offering of incense, and pray to Hekate. The statue is now charged with her energy and acts as a direct channel to her.

CHAPTER 7

SPIRITUAL BATHS

To prepare oneself for magick, it is essential that one be pure and clean, bathing at intervals.

—LORD CORVUS OF THESSALLY

Before all magick or ritual is performed, it is necessary to bathe properly. The bath has the dual purpose of both removing unwanted spiritual vibration and infusing the witch with the power/vibration that is sought. This is done by placing various herbs and/or oils in the bath and then pouring this mixture over yourself.

CONCERNING THE PREPARATION OF THE BATH

Before you take a spiritual bath, you must first clean the tub in which the bath is to be taken. This is done by adding a capful of ammonia to a gallon of water and scrubbing the tub down. Ammonia is used because it has the magical quality of removing any unwanted energy, both good and bad, from an object or dwelling. By washing the tub with the ammonia and water mixture, you are basically wiping the slate clean and neutralizing the energies that may be associated with the tub.

With this accomplished, you need to next fill the tub up with water. The faucet water is fine, as it will be magically cleansed and consecrated prior to use. Water for a spiritual bath should be as cold as the person bathing can stand it. A good temperature is 65 to 70 degrees. To this bath water add 3 tablespoons of sea salt and 1 tablespoon of baking soda. Place the tip of your athame into the water and say:

I exorcise thee O' Creature of Water. Let all malignity and hindrance be cast forth hence from, and let all good enter herein. In the names of the Great Mother and Father Gods do I purify, bless, and invoke thee.

Trace an invoking pentagram on the surface of the water using the wand or index finger of your power hand.

At this point, the water is purified and charged to neutralize and cleanse the aura of the person bathing. Now all that remains is to add the proper potion to infuse the water with the energy desired. This is done by adding a tea made of specific herbs that are in harmony with the task at hand.

CONCERNING BATH TEAS

Following is a list of several bath teas that can be used for different types of magick. *Under no circumstances are you to drink any of these teas!* To make your bath teas, use about a teaspoon of each herb to a pint or more of boiling water. It is best to use a large, mesh, tea ball, available at most grocery stores, for making these teas. Bring your water to a boil and then turn off the heat. Place the herbs into the water, cover, and let steep for about five minutes.

Place 1 cup of the bath tea into the water and enter the tub. Kneel in the water, which should reach up to your waist, and with a small bucket or large cup begin to scoop up the water and pour it over your head and body. Make very certain that you are completely doused with the water.

While you are pouring the bath water over you, you must visualize yourself as being cleansed and empowered. It is also very important to chant a rhythmic chant stating the purpose of the bath while dousing yourself. For the best effect, say the chant and then pour the water over you. Repeat this for several minutes. When done, step out of the bath and dry yourself with a clean white towel. If you work sky-clad, (i.e., naked) proceed to the ritual area; if you work robed, now is the time to dress and go to your ritual area.

Below is a list of various baths and chants that can be used for different types of magick. One again, never drink any of the teas for these baths.

Love Drawing Bath

Use this bath prior to performing any type of ritual or spell to attract love for yourself or rekindle love in a present relationship. For this bath, make a tea of equal parts:

- Lavender
- Rose petals
- Rosemary

Add 1 cup of the tea to the bath water and chant:

Love, happiness, and sexuality;
I call you all to come to me.

Purification Bath

Use this bath prior to any type of high Magick or when you feel you have picked up a lot of negative energy that must be disposed of. For this bath, make a tea of equal parts:

- Frankincense
- Myrrh
- Vervain
- Hyssop
- Basil

Add 1 cup of the tea to the bath water and chant:

Water mixed with herbs of power
banish from me all things sour.

Power Bath

Use this bath prior to performing magick. It cleanses and infuses the body and aura and allows power to flow more easily. Works extremely well. For this bath, make a tea of equal parts:

- Ginger
- Solomon's seal
- Mandrake

Add 1 cup of the tea to the bath water and chant:

Herbs of magick; grant me power
increase my magick this day and this hour.

Circle Bath

Use this bath prior to attending a ritual or Sabbat circle. This bath allows your energy to mingle more readily with other people's, thus making group power-raising more effective. For this bath, make a tea of equal parts:

- Rosemary
- Myrrh
- Sandalwood
- Frankincense

Add 1 cup of the tea to the bath water and chant:

Round the witches' circle go,
Feel the power, let it go.

Hex-Breaking Bath

Bathe in this to break or remove heavy negative influences or the spells of another that may have been cast on you. When finished, shower or bathe with fresh clean water. For this bath, make a tea of equal parts:

- Frankincense
- Rosemary
- Sandalwood
- add 9 cloves to the tea

Add 1 cup of the tea to the bath water and chant:

Evil, Harm, Negativity
From my life banished be.

Protection Bath

Bathe to protect yourself from all psychic attack. Very effective. For this bath, make a tea of equal parts:

- Frankincense
- Dragon's blood
- Myrrh
- Salt

Add 1 cup of this tea to the bath water and chant:

> *A Wall of fire around me is twined*
> *Protection and safety now are mine.*

Four Elements Bath

Bathe with this mixture to bring yourself into balance and remove deception, both from yourself and others. For this bath make a tea of equal parts:

- Patchouli
- Anise
- Angelica
- Chamomile

Add 1 cup of this tea to the bath water and chant:

> *Earth and Air; Fire and Water, Surround me with protective Light*
> *Earth and Air; Fire and Water, Guard me with your magical might.*

Divination Bath

Use this bath prior to very important divination. Be very certain to wash the back of the neck thoroughly with this wash. This allows your inner spirit to express itself more freely. For this bath make a tea of equal parts:

- Wormwood
- Mugwort
- Rue

Add 1 cup of this tea to the bath water and chant:

Herbs of magick on this night
grant me now the second sight.

Water Bath

Use this bath when you feel you need more water energy to help balance you. This bath infuses you with the power of the element water. For this bath make a tea of equal parts:

- Chamomile
- Geranium
- Sandalwood

Add 1 cup of the tea to the bath water and chant:

Water spirits, Western Undines,
Gather round and add thy power to mine.

Fire Bath

Use this bath when you need extra energy to do work or to balance yourself if you lack the fire element. This bath infuses you with the elemental power of fire. For this bath make a tea of equal parts:

- Orange Peel
- Juniper
- Frankincense
- Basil

Add 1 cup of the tea to the bath water and chant:

Salamanders, Southern Spirits bright
Join me now upon this night.

Earth Bath

Use this bath to attune you to the element earth or to ground yourself after performing magick. For this bath make a tea of equal parts:

- Patchouli
- Cypress
- Vetiver

Add one cup of the tea to the bath water and chant:

> *Gnomes of Earth, Spirits of North,*
> *Come to me, I call thee forth.*

Air Bath

Use this bath to help attune you to the element and powers of air. It is useful prior to any type of studying or creative endeavor. For this bath make a tea of equal parts:

- Lavender
- Rosemary
- Mint

Add 1 cup of this tea to the bath water and chant:

> *Spirits of East, Sylphs so fair,*
> *Attend me here, your magick do share.*

Invisibility Bath

Use this bath when you are performing magick on others and do not wish to be discovered through divination or any other means. For this bath make a tea of equal parts:

- Fern
- Mistletoe
- Poppy seeds
- add 3 drops of pine essential oil to the bath water

Add one cup of the tea to the bath water and chant:

Lord and Lady by your power and might,
shield me round and keep me from sight.

Magical Eye Bath. For this one you will need to make a strong decoction of the herb called eyebright. To make the decoction, just add three teaspoons of the herb to a pint of water and boil it down until it is about a cup of water. Strain the herb out and allow the decoction to cool.

Next, pour some distilled water into a large clean bowl (mixing bowls work great). Pour enough water so that you can submerge your face into the water. Add the eyebright decoction to this water and dunk you face down into the bowl.

When your face is in the water, open your eyes and rotate them around. This may sting at first, but soon you will become accustomed to it. This magical eye bath leaves the eyes clean and shiny and also aids in the seeing of spirits and fairies.

CHAPTER 8

HERBS AND THEIR USES

...and you, Earth, who teaches the
potency of Herbs...

—OVID, *METAMORPHOSES*

CONCERNING THE USE
OF HERBS FOR HEALTH AND HEALING

A witch is not only a magical practitioner, but also a healer. Healing can be performed in two ways. You can heal by use of magical means or you can heal by use of herbs and potions. Simple illnesses like a cold, influenza, gout, fevers, and skin irritations can be healed quite easily with the application of special herbal concoctions.

It is important for you to know that should a client come to you with a medical problem you cannot, by law, administer the concoction. You can instruct the client in the making of the potion, but you cannot make and administer it. The laws may vary from state to state, so it would be wise to check these local laws. Believe me, if the doctors in your area find out that your potions are doing better than their medicines, they will take you to court, and you could be slapped with a huge fine and perhaps put in jail. So abide by local laws. You also cannot legally diagnose an illness if you are not a certified doctor of medicine. The safest avenue to take is to ask clients if they have first consulted a physician. If they have not, then recommend that they do before you perform any type of physical healing.

For yourself or for close friends and coveners, there should be no problem. While these laws may seem unfair to our kind, they are truly for the safety and security of the public as a whole. After all, anyone can read a book about herbal healing and then try to experiment on their clients without ever having tried them first.

Another problem that I have seen is that many people seem to feel that herbal remedies are completely safe to take in any combination or quantity because they are all natural. This is a deadly and dangerous way of thinking. Many herbs can be lethal in large doses, and any herbal potion should be treated with the same respect as a prescription drug.

Following are 10 common ailments that I often treat in my family, my students, and myself. I give the name of the ailment, the symptoms and the recipe that I administer to cure it. These remedies are safe and very effective. They have worked, in many cases, where pharmaceutical medicines have failed. Use with caution and follow all directions exactly. The use of these potions is entirely up to you, and I accept no responsibility for any adverse effects that may result from their use or misuse.

Acute Bronchitis

Causes and Symptoms. Bronchitis is caused by a virus or bacteria that affects the mucous membrane lining in the bronchial tubes. This virus causes large amounts of mucous, called phlegm, to be formed. Often, the virus or bacteria will spread down into the lungs causing much coughing.

Symptoms include fever, chills, and a continuous coughing, especially in the early morning. Coughing usually expels small amounts of phlegm. After a time, larger amounts of phlegm begin to be expelled. In children, there is the danger of suffocation or choking on this phlegm. When suffering from bronchitis, you should lie down on your side, not your back, to avoid choking.

Treatment: Yellow Dock Syrup
    ½ pound yellow dock root
    1 pint distilled water
    ½ cup dark honey
    ½ cup molasses
    1 tbsp. pure maple syrup
    a dash of pure vanilla extract

Boil the yellow dock root in the pint of distilled water. *Do not* use any aluminum pots for this. Enamel-coated pots or Pyrex are the best to use, as metal tends to destroy the essential oils of the herbs used. Boil the root until the liquid is reduced to about 1 cup.

Strain the root out and to this liquid add the rest of the ingredients. This will make a heavy syrup. Bottle and label. Make sure to put the date that you made this syrup, as it will only keep for one year if refrigerated.

To administer, take one teaspoon at a time for bronchitis. This syrup is my most popular recipe and is highly effective. It also works quite well for those suffering with emphysema to help in breathing.

Common Cold

Causes and Symptoms. The cause of the common cold is identical to bronchitis, except that the infection lies in the throat.

The symptoms of a cold are also identical to bronchitis. However, when one has a cold, fevers tend to be more prominent and the coughing not quite as severe. A sore or scratchy throat is often present and the stomach will often hurt when one coughs.

Treatment: Cinnamon Cold and Flu Cure
> 2 cups distilled water
> 1 cinnamon stick
> 4 cloves
> 2 tsp lemon juice (freshly squeezed)
> 1½ tbsp. honey
> 2 tbsp. of brandy

Boil the cinnamon stick and cloves together in the 2 cups of distilled water for about three minutes. Remove from heat and add the rest of the ingredients. Stir well, cover, and let stand for twenty minutes. After twenty minutes, strain and bottle.

This remedy should be used immediately and should not be stored. To administer it, drink ½ cup every three to four hours until completely gone. It tastes great and works very well at breaking up congestion and fevers that accompany the common cold or flu. It should be drunk hot; so once it cools, feel free to reheat before drinking.

Constipation and Diarrhea

Causes and Symptoms. Constipation is the result of improper diet. Too much meat and excessive amounts of liquor and pharmaceutical drugs can also result in constipation. Irregular bowel habits can also contribute to constipation. Diarrhea is caused by large amounts of fluids in the system.

Constipation is accompanied by difficulty and pain when having a bowel movement. Often, constipation can result in headaches, fevers, and severe abdominal cramps. Diarrhea is the exact opposite. It is excessive and watery bowel excretions. If not treated, diarrhea can result in dehydration.

Treatment: Blackberry Syrup. This treatment is wonderful in the fact that it treats both constipation and diarrhea. Sounds unusual, but it works quite well.

> 1 tsp. allspice
> 1 cup unsweetened blackberry juice

Pour the blackberry juice into a saucepan and put on low heat. Place the allspice in a cheesecloth bag and then put the bag into the blackberry juice. Simmer for about two minutes. Remove the allspice bag and allow the juice to cool. Bottle and label; then keep refrigerated.

To administer, take one tablespoon of the syrup every four hours. Symptoms should clear up within twenty-four hours.

Minor Burns

Causes and Symptoms. Minor burns occur most often in the kitchen. Hot grease splattering, hot water burns, or grabbing a pot off the stove without thinking.

A minor burn will quickly turn the skin red, and a blister may form within seconds. It is accompanied by a continuous burning sensation at the area of the burn, which will continue until treated.

Treatment: Soy Sauce. For minor burns that result in the kitchen, simply apply soy sauce directly to the burn as soon as possible. This will stop the burning sensation and prevent blistering. Do not, as is commonly thought, run the burn under cold water. This will only serve to increase the blistering and could result in a scar.

Minor Cuts and Abrasions

Causes and Symptoms. We all, from time to time, accidentally cut ourselves. A minor cut is classified as one that does not break too far into the skin. A cut down to the bone is not a minor cut.

A minor cut will, of course, be painful and will be followed with a slight issuance of blood. When you cut yourself, it is important to let the blood flow for several seconds before stopping it. The reason for this is because the rushing out of the blood will wash away much of the infectious bacteria usually associated with cuts. Once the bleeding is checked, you should begin treatment.

Treatment: Juniper Berry Tea.
> 9 tbsp of juniper berries
> 1 quart distilled water

Place the berries and water in a pot and bring to a boil. Turn off the flame and let steep for one hour.

To administer this treatment, simply wash the wound three times a day with this tea. Results will be seen within one to two days. The rate of healing is increased by this formula, and infection is removed and/or prevented.

Excessive Menstruation

Causes and Symptoms. Profuse menstruation can be caused by any number of things, including an imbalance of the hormones, a deficiency of iron in the blood, metabolic diseases, and many others. If menstruation is continuously excessive, consult a doctor, as serious loss of blood can be life threatening.

If the flow of menstrual blood is excessive, but not extremely so, try this treatment. Other symptoms are weakness, headaches, and moodiness.

Treatment: Proper Diet and Bayberry Bark . Avoid all alcoholic beverages, as alcohol thins the blood and will only make things worse. Also avoid any spicy foods. Eat plenty of fruits and vegetables. Take bayberry bark capsules until menses has stopped; then make a tea of bayberry bark and white oak bark.

> 5 tbsp bayberry bark
> 5 tbsp white oak bark
> 1 quart distilled water

Add the herbs to the water and bring to a boil. Remove from heat and let steep for fifteen minutes. Use this tea as a douche, once it has cooled. This will promote internal healing and prevent future excessive menstruation.

Chicken Pox

Causes and Symptoms. Chicken Pox is caused by a virus that is highly contagious. While chicken pox can be a serious illness, if properly cared for, it heals quickly. It is most common in young children. Once you have gotten chicken pox, you develop an immunity to the virus and will never get it again.

The symptoms of chicken pox are easily identified. The skin becomes covered with small red sores that usually first appear around the wrists and face. Exposure to sunlight will irritate the sores and can lead to scarring. Fever is also a common symptom, along with tiredness, headache, and vomiting and itching.

Treatment: Dock Root Tea. To relieve the itching of the sores associated with chicken pox and to prevent any scarring, nothing works better than yellow dock tea.

> 1 lb yellow dock root.
> 1 quart distilled water

121

Add the root to the water and bring to a boil. Remove from the heat and allow to cool.

The tea should be used to wash the body. For the best results, give an oatmeal bath (available at any drug store) and then apply the dock root tea using a face towel. For best results, apply the tea while it is still warm, but not hot. This may initially cause the sores to itch more, but when the skin cools the itching will stop completely.

The sores are light sensitive, so the patient should remain in bed and all sunlight and even electric lights should be blocked out as much as possible. The diet of the patient should consist of vegetable broths, fruit juices, and hot cereals such as oatmeal. Results will be seen in just a day or two.

Nervous Headaches

Causes and Symptoms. This type of headache is usually caused when a person is under tremendous stress or during times of great concern over how or why something is happening.

This headache is easily determined, because the situations going on that promote this type of headache are the key factor. Also, any loud noises or bright lights will tend to worsen the pain of these headaches.

Treatment: Chamomile Tea. This is one of the best headache treatments I have ever used. Chamomile tea is effective because it relaxes the body and the mind. It is a soothing tea and it will calm the nerves, thus curing the cause of the headache.

To make a good chamomile tea, steep 2 tablespoons of fresh or dried flowers in a quart of water for forty minutes. To administer this cure, simply pour yourself a cup of the tea, sweeten it with dark honey or pure maple syrup and drink 2 cups per day.

Sick Headache

Causes and Symptoms. This type of headache usually results when the body is recovering from an illness. The headache is caused by a lack of iron in the blood. This headache can also be caused from liver disorders or when a person is physically or mentally overworked.

The symptoms of this headache are similar to those of a nervous headache, but this type is more of a throbbing pain that seems centered in the forehead and temples.

Treatment: Hot Footbath and Spearmint Tea. To get relief from this type of headache, all you need to do is add 1 tablespoon of mustard seed to a hot footbath. The water should be as hot as the patient can stand it. Place a cold washcloth on the forehead.

Also drink 1 cup of spearmint tea. To make this tea, put 2 tablespoons of fresh or dried herb to 1 quart of water. Bring to a boil and let steep for fifteen minutes. Sweeten with honey.

Poison Ivy

Causes and Symptoms. Exposure to a plant of the sumac family— poison ivy, poison oak, or poison sumac—will cause the skin to become slightly swollen and covered with clusters of tiny blisters. The most common places for these blisters are the face, between the fingers, arms, and hands. In severe cases, blistering may result in permanent scarring. The blisters are accompanied by intense itching and irritation.

Treatment: Acorn Tea and Hot Water. To treat the infection of poison ivy or poison oak, gather up a dozen or so acorns and crack them open. Put them in 1 quart of distilled water and bring to a boil. Let it boil until the water is reduced to one half of the original liquid. Wash the blistered areas with this tea, or, if possible, soak the area in this tea.

The high tannin content of the acorns will effectively dry up the blisters, causing them to flake away in just a matter of days.

To stop the intense itching of poison ivy or poison oak, simply run the affected area under very hot water. While under the water, the itching will increase, but keep it under the hot water until it stops. When you remove it from the water, the area will be itch-free for up to an hour or more. If you cannot soak the area in hot water or run hot water over it, simply set your hair dryer on maximum heat and blow the hot air onto the affected part for the same results.

Fevers

Causes and Symptoms. Fevers are caused by infections in the body. These infections are usually caused by a virus or bacteria that has entered the body.

Symptoms include headaches, increased body temperature, and vomiting.

Treatment: Yarrow and Ginger Tea with a Cold Compress. Make a tea of yarrow herb and ginger root. To make this tea, add 1 tablespoon of yarrow and ½ tablespoon of ground ginger root to a pint of boiling water. Let it steep for twenty minutes and drink 1 cup every hour.

To make a cold compress, simply take a small face towel or washcloth and soak it in cold water. Place this on the forehead of the sick person to help lower his or her fever. Sometimes, the cold compress alone will give wonderful relief to a person suffering from fever.

CONCERNING THE USE OF HERBS FOR MAGICK

The spiritual law of analogy teaches us that all things in life are interconnected, beyond separation. It is this law that opens up the door to the use of various natural items to bring about certain types of energy.

All that exists does so at a certain vibrational frequency. Some items vibrate at the same frequency as others, thus making them emit the same type of energy.

For example, the Moon emits an energy vibrating at a certain frequency, which affects us in many different ways. The herb mugwort vibrates at the same vibrational frequency, or close to it. Thus, mugwort can be used to bring in the energies of the Moon, even when the Moon is not visible. Ingesting a tea made of mugwort would infuse your entire body with the vibrations of the Moon!

The same applies for any other herb or object. Before making teas with any herb, be certain that it is not poisonous. Below is a list of common herbs used by witches and the ways in which to use them.

Rue - Rue is used in any type of uncrossing or unhexing incense or washes. If you feel that you are the victim of the evil eye, a pinch of rue placed on the tongue will break this infamous curse. Be prepared, however; rue is considered the bitterest herb in the world. Rue placed inside of a small red cloth bag and worn or carried on the body promotes healing.

Fennel - Fennel seeds are carried for the purpose of keeping away evil spirits. It is very effective in this capacity. To do this, place some fennel seeds, vervain, and frankincense into a small red cloth bag and carry it with you.

Vervain - Vervain is often used to promote a peaceful energy in a home. The popular floor wash, called Juno's Tears or Juno's Brew, which is used to banish a restless spirit or to bring peace to a home, has as its main ingredient, Vervain. Vervain is also used in many love spells and incense mixtures designed to bring love.

Wormwood - An incense of wormwood and sandalwood is often burned in order to allow the spirits of the dead to speak. This is best performed through the use of a skrying mirror or bowl. If you call upon the name of the person you wish to contact and then gaze into the mirror of water, the person's face should appear in the skrying tool and begin to speak.

In times past, wormwood was the main ingredient in an alcoholic beverage called absinthe. Absinthe was banned in most countries due to its alleged side effects to a person's physical health. Through my research, however, I find that the damaging effects of absinthe are nothing more than the same physical ailments inherent in any person who suffers from chronic alcoholism. Absinthe was said to be an aphrodisiac and a powerful catalyst to stimulate the creative mind. Today, there are many who are lobbying to have the laws against absinthe revoked.

Frankincense - The most famous and certainly most used herb in the world. Frankincense is actually the resin from a tree that grows in Europe. The resin of this tree was so valued that, in ancient times, the Egyptian queen Hapshetsut launched a large expedition to travel by boat out to the land of Punt just to bring back frankincense trees and other exotic items. Frankincense, when burned, will chase away all negativity and evil from an area, leaving a very calm and uplifting vibration within the room. Thus it is used in nearly every type of purification and exorcism incense. Frankincense is also one of the main ingredients in the incense used by the Catholic Church.

Myrrh - Myrrh is burned for much the same reasons as frankincense— to clear the area of unwanted negativity and promote peace. However, myrrh is rarely burned alone. It is best to combine myrrh with frankincense for a more powerful incense. The reason for this is that frankincense is a masculine herb while myrrh is a feminine herb. Thus the two combined create a very balanced energy of lord and lady and as any witch knows, balance is the key to success in all things.

Benzoin - This is an excellent clearing incense. Burn this when your mind is cluttered and you cannot find a direction to go in. Mixed with cinnamon and burned in a place of business, it will bring customers to your door.

Cinquefoil - More commonly known as five-finger grass because its leaves come to five points. The points represent money, power, wisdom, love, and health. In my practices, I have found myself using cinquefoil nearly as much as frankincense. Cinquefoil has the magical property of allowing a person to speak fluently and with eloquence. Used in spells for court proceedings, it is unsurpassed in its effectiveness to help win the favor of a judge or jury. An infusion of cinquefoil added to the bathwater can help to break spells cast against you.

Mandrake - The most magical of all herbs, mandrake is all but impossible to find today. What most occult shops sell as mandrake is actually the American version of Mandrake, the mayapple. True mandrake grows in Europe, and the root is large and roughly shaped like a human being. Mandrake was considered to be so magical, that a special ritual was needed to extract it from the ground. First, the witch would have to stop up his or her ears with wax, because it was believed that mandrake, when pulled from the ground, would emit a scream that would kill anyone who heard it. Second, the witch had to tie one end of a rope around the plant and the other end around a white dog. The witch would then throw some food or a bone for the dog to fetch. When the dog ran to get the food, it would pull the root out of the ground. At this point, the witch would blow a horn very loudly so as to help drown out the shrieking that the plant made. Only then could the root be used.

There are literally hundreds of magical uses for mandrake. The most popular of which is its use in love potions, particularly rituals designed to increase sexual drive and release inhibitions. This is probably due to the psychotropic effects the mandrake has if taken internally. However, mandrake is extremely toxic, and if one does not know the exact proportions to take, it will cause death. Do not attempt to eat or drink anything that contains mandrake. The mere presence of mandrake will chase away any negative spirits, and it can be used in small portions to add power to any other incense.

Rose Petals - Roses have always been the universal symbol of love. These flowers are sacred to Aphrodite herself. Scatter rose petals under the pillow of the one you love to cause him or her to dream of you. Place the name of the one you love beneath a pink candle and circle it with red or pink rose petals to bring out their love for you. Also, rose petals can be made into a type of candy that can be eaten by two lovers to help bring out more of their love.

To make the candy, separate 7 egg whites from the yolks and add 7 tablespoons of sugar. With an eggbeater, whip the whites until they form a thick meringue. With a small pastry brush, lightly brush the meringue onto some large rose petals. Allow them to dry; then turn them over and brush the other side. When they are completely dry, they will have the consistency of a hard candy. These can be eaten to increase love in a marriage or relationship. This should be done when the couple is alone in the house and by candlelight, perhaps as the dessert to a nice dinner at home.

Balm of Gilead - This is not an herb, per se, but actually the buds of the poplar tree. The effects of balm of Gilead are quite amazing, when taken as a tea. (See the dream tea in chapter 9. Magically, balm of Gilead is burned as an incense. The smoke of the burning balm is said to be a wonderful basis in which spirits or entities can materialize. I can vouch for the effectiveness of this particular use of the plant. Simply place two or three buds onto a lit charcoal and call the name of the spirit three times. Watch the smoke carefully, and in a short time you will see a shape take form. There is nothing to fear about negative entities, as balm of Gilead is also a protective herb that will banish negative energy. However, to be safe, call only spirits that are readily helpful and who are beneficial. This method is especially effective when dealing with spirits of the air and water elements.

Belladonna - This herb, sometimes called nightshade, has a long history of magical use. The priests of the goddess Bellona would drink an infusion of this herb prior to her worship. This is because the plant is highly psychotropic, and also extremely poisonous. Do not drink any infusions of this herb unless you know what you are doing. Accidental poisonings that lead to death are not uncommon even today.

A better alternative use for belladonna is as an incense, and it should only be burned outdoors over a fire. This herb is virtually impossible to buy, so you may need to learn how to identify it. It grows in nearly every state in the United States and is commonly found in wooded areas that border highways.

If you have some, dry it and grind it in your mortar for toxic herbs. Next, take several handfuls of the ground herb and head out to a secluded area of the woods on the night of the new moon. Light a small fire and allow it to burn down to glowing embers. Take a handful of the dried belladonna and toss it onto the glowing coals. Say the following chant:

Herb of Night; Herb of Shade
Power come as this charge is made.
By Hekate's power do I ask.
To grant my wish 'ere this night is past.
By the power of the Nightshade plant,

I ask of thee, my wish to grant.
By the power of Hekate three;
As I will so shall it be.

Take a symbol of your desire and hold it within the rising smoke. *Be certain that you do not breath in the smoke.* Now turn and move to the nearest tree and bury the symbol at its base. Make certain that the fire is out and leave the area without looking back. In this way, will your wish be granted.

Hemlock - This herb is probably most famous for its use as a form of execution in ancient Greece. The famous philosopher Socrates was condemned to drink an infusion of hemlock as punishment for his supposed crimes. Hemlock has long been used for magical purposes. Hemlock when combined with black poppy seeds can be burned as an incense that will call forth spirits (this should only be done outdoors). But probably the most effective use of hemlock would be for the anointing of magical blades.

To do this, first locate a live hemlock plant. You can find them growing on the sides of country roads and roads that are not heavily traveled and where water is plentiful. When you find one, draw a circle around the plant on the ground. After this you should tap the stalk of the herb three times with your knife and then cut it down with one stroke. If the plant is large, as this plant can often be, you can take a sprig from atop the plant.

When you have your hemlock, return home with it and begin the process. First, sprinkle the herb with consecrated water and fumigate it with a mixture of frankincense and myrrh. This will purify it and cleanse it of any negative vibrations. Next, take up your magical blade, be it athame or sword, into your left hand and, using your right hand, pass the hemlock, over the blade. Start this process as a gentle sweeping motion as you begin to chant:

Hemlock gathered from the wild,
I (your magical name), *am the Old Ones' child.*
Thy powers of magick do I command
To bless this blade within my hand.
With thy magick juice do I anoint
From hilt to guard and then to point.
Within this blade, spirits will I see;
As I will so shall it be.

Take a leaf from the plant and rub it vigorously onto the blade on both sides until the blade is moist with the juice of the hemlock. Wrap the knife up in a black cloth and store it away until your next ritual. It is said that a blade anointed in such a way will act as a magical mirror, allowing the person holding the knife to see spirits in the reflections on the metal blade. This works quite well and can be very useful when trying to perform any type of banishing ritual.

Holy Thistle - Often called blessed thistle, this herb is used in magical operations that are designed to promote healing and prosperity. It can be made into a green blood and washed over a person to break any hexes or curses with which the person may be afflicted (see p. 132, Concerning the Green Blood). A bowl of thistle leaves placed into a room or a live potted thistle will bring peace to a home.

Yellow Dock - This vibrant plant is a nuisance plant for those who try to keep a well-managed lawn. However, the dock plant is useful both medicinally and magically, and witches find themselves using it again and again. The root of the plant can be grated and boiled into a tea that is used for money drawing baths or rituals. The leaves can be used for the same. The seeds of the dock make an extremely effective money incense. Medicinally, dock root is good for colds and any type of bronchial trouble.

Camphor - Associated with the moon, camphor can be burned in conjunction with jasmine as one of the most effective moon incenses I have ever used. I have also used camphor successfully as a healing and purification incense. Real camphor is difficult to obtain in some areas; if you have trouble finding it, there are some effective synthetics on the market. However, actual camphor is preferred.

Dragon's Blood - In my opinion, this is the most effective hex-breaking agent in existence. Dragon's blood, when placed in any other incense, strengthens and increases the power of that incense. Burned in conjunction with other purification herbs, it renders a person impervious to any psychic attack, be it from witch or spirit.

CONCERNING THE GREEN BLOOD

Green blood is a catchall term for a very powerful fluid condenser created by the ripping and tearing of fresh herbs in water while chanting, empowering, and charging the condenser.

In the making of the green blood *only* fresh herbs are to be used. Gather them yourself and take them home. Place the herbs in their own separate piles on your altar or ancestor shrine. Place a mixture of frankincense and myrrh upon a lit charcoal. Waft the smoke over the herbs to purify them. Next, sprinkle some consecrated water over the herbs to consecrate them.

Pour 1 gallon of distilled or spring water into a large bucket. Place the herbs into the water and lower the tips of your fingers into the water. Begin chanting as you slowly start to tear the herbs. Remember to push the herbs under the water as you shred them. As your chant builds and the power rises, begin to chant and tear faster. Do this for several minutes or until the water has become dark green in color.

You now have the green blood. It is charged with your power as well as the powers of the herbs associated with your desire and is extremely powerful.

The Uses of the Green Blood

Green blood can be used just as you would any oil or wash. The difference is that green blood cannot be stored. It must all be used immediately.

Use green blood to ritually cleanse yourself when performing outdoor rituals and an actual ritual bath is not possible.

Place some of the green blood in your mop water and wash down the floors and walls of your home or business to attract or repel the energy of your choice.

Put some of the green blood in a bowl and using your fingers or an asperser sprinkle about your home or business to attract or repel as needed. A good asperser can be made from sprigs of fresh herbs or leaves from a tree. Bundle them together and dip them into the green blood and sprinkle about.

Place some of the green blood in your bath (strain first) and use to draw or repel your desired effect.

Below is a list of various recipes for different types of green blood.

Purification
- Mimosa
- Elder leaves
- Hyssop

> Chant: *Herbs of three in here are placed;*
> *Negativity be displaced.*

Healing
- Mint
- Rosemary
- Marjoram

   Chant: *Herbs of magick, thy power I use;*
   Healing energy I here infuse.

Hex-Breaking
- Datura leaves (use caution)
- Hydrangea
- Elder leaves

   Chant: *By the powers of magick in me,*
   Completely cleansed and uncrossed I be.

Legal Matters (to gain favor in)
- Marigold
- Cabbage
- Fern

   Chant: *Friendly judge, to you I hail;*
   Fairness and Justice shall prevail.

Love
- Chamomile
- Clover
- Jasmine flowers

   Chant: *Love is the bond, and love is the Law;*
   By this magick, Love to me I draw.

To See Who Loves You
- St. John's wort
- Rose petal
- Willow leaves

Chant: *By magick infusion and witch's rite,*
In dreams I see who loves me this night.

To Break Love Spells
- Lily
- Lotus
- 3 pistachio nuts

Chant: *A spell of love on me has been cast,*
By this bath, this love is now past.

To Bring luck
- Daffodil
- Oak leaves
- Leek

Chant: *Luck and Prosperity,*
Flow into my life that be.

To Strengthen Mental Powers
- Rue
- Rosemary
- Spearmint

Chant: *Magick Spearmint, Rosemary, and Rue;*
Strengthen my mind in all I do.

To Bring Money
- Yellow dock leaves
- Elder flowers
- Mint

Chant: *Money, money come to me;*
As I will, so mote it be.

Power
- Carnations
- Spanish moss
- Oak leaves

   Chant: *Herbs of grace, I call upon thee in this hour;*
   Grant me all of thy blessed power.

Prosperity
- Tulip petals
- Oak leaves
- Ash leaves

   Chant: *Luck and Prosperity,*
   Flow into my life that be.

Protection
- African violet (leaves and flowers)
- Broom or broom tops
- Elder leaves

   Chant: *All that is harmful and negative must go;*
   Protection around, above and below.

Psychic Powers
- Grass
- Rue
- Wormwood

   Chant: *Psychic powers to me bring;*
   Beauty bright in everything.

To Call Spirits
- Dandelion
- Tobacco

- Wormwood

  Chant: *By powerful magick and mystical spell,*
  Spirits I conjure, and may they speed well.

Success (to bring)
- Clover
- Lemon peel
- Oak leaves

  Chant: ~~*This spell I cast to do me well;*~~
  Success is mine by this my spell.

To Prevent Theft
- Juniper leaves and berries
- Wormwood
- Rue

  Chant: *Thief, your eye will never shine*
  On these beloved things of mine.

(Sprinkle the mixture onto the objects to be protected.)

CONCERNING INCENSE AND FUMIGATIONS

The use of incense in ritual dates back to the far reaches of human history. Who can deny that certain smells conjure up both good and bad feelings or memories. This is because the olfactory gland, the gland in charge of the sense of smell, is directly linked to the parts of the brain where both our short- and long-term memories are stored. Thus, certain smells will recall certain memories. It is for this reason that so many different blends of incense are used in rituals.

It is very important that you remain consistent with the types of incense that you use when you are performing your rituals. For example, you should have a special blend for your meditations, a blend for your full moon rituals, a blend for your new moon rituals, a blend for each Sabbat, a blend for Esbats, a divination incense, and a general-use blend.

The use of these various scents is of the utmost importance. By using a certain incense for a specific ritual, you are in actuality training your mind and your memory. Through prolonged use of the specific incense for the specific rite, over time you will, simply by smelling the incense, come to the proper state of mind for the ritual at hand. This is particularly true of meditation. With prolonged use, you will only need to light the incense and assume your meditative posture, and the scent will immediately bring you into your calm and meditative mind.

The "Smoke Bath"

This type of "bath" is a fumigation, using herbs and/or a special incense blend. This is most commonly done after a special bath to first clean the aura, and then the smoke is used to charge the aura with the desired energy. To perform it is quite simple.

ITEMS NEEDED

- Chair
- Censer and charcoal
- Heavy blanket or sheet
- Incense or herb to be used

Place the censer with the lit charcoal in it beneath the chair. Now place the incense blend or herb onto the charcoal so that it begins to smoke. Quickly seat yourself in the chair and wrap the blanket or sheet over your shoulders, covering your body and the chair. It is helpful to have an assistant go around and make certain there are no gaps in the bottom of the sheet. Make sure that the sheet reaches the floor.

The idea is to trap the smoke within the blanket, thus containing it and fumigating, or "bathing" the body in the smoke. It is best to be sky-clad (naked) beneath the sheet so that the smoke has direct contact with the skin. However, if in the company of others and you are shy, you can wear just your underclothes or perhaps a bathing suit.

A few rules are to be followed when performing a smoke bath. First, never place your head under the sheet. The smoke can cause severe bronchial trouble. Second, if you have asthma or any respiratory problems, do not perform a smoke bath. Simply take a second "activating" spiritual bath. Third, never use herbs that are toxic for a smoke bath. Why? Because you might die. If you wish to experiment, be certain that you research very carefully and if in doubt, ask someone who is a professional.

Some Incense Blends

Below is a list of incense blends that can be used to enhance your practices and to honor holy days. These are just guides; experiment and research to find the scent that best suits you.

Incense for Magical Practice

Divination Incense
- Flaxseed
- Fleabane
- Violet root
- Parsley

Full Moon Incense
- Camphor
- Lemon peel
- Powdered benzoin

Noumenia (New Moon) Incense
- Verbena
- Pine
- Frankincense
- Patchouli

Ritual Incense
- Rosemary
- Verbena

General Magick Incense
- Frankincense
- Myrrh
- Copal

Protection Incense
- Frankincense
- Myrrh
- Dragon's blood

Incense for Holy Days

Thargelia (Beltane, May 1st) Incense
- Frankincense
- Sandalwood
- Rose petals

Kronia (Imbolc, February 2nd) Incense
- Dragon's blood

Herbs and Their Uses

- Cinnamon
- Frankincense

Elusinia (Lughnasah) Incense
- Frankincense
- Lavender
- Pinch of saffron

Dionysia (Mabon) Incense
- Crushed oak leaves
- Cypress
- Juniper

Pan-festival (Midsummer) Incense
- Frankincense
- Benzoin
- Sandalwood

Anthesteria (Ostara) Incense
- Rose petals
- Nutmeg
- Orange peels

Thesmophoria (Samhain) Incense
- Brown Sugar
- Patchouli
- Frankincense

Haloa (Yule) Incense
- Frankincense
- Pine
- Cedar

Before you begin blending incense it is important that you concentrate on the reason that you are doing it. Focus your attention on the purpose at hand and chant the following:

> *Herbs of Magick do I mix*
> *for* (state purpose) *these herbs I fix.*
> *An incense of mystic scent I blend*
> *Its power to my magick lend.*

CONCERNING MAGICAL PROTECTION

When I first became involved in magical practices, I began with ceremonial magick. I quickly learned that magical protection is of the utmost importance when practicing and working in magical ways. This is because when performing ritual, the energy that you raise is very attractive to a variety of spirits, and they will come and huddle around, waiting to absorb that energy and thereby gain strength.

More often than not you will have little or no trouble from these spirits, other than an occasional glimpse of them out the corner of your eye or some small objects missing from your house, only to resurface in some unusual place. I have adopted the name "Little Nasties" for them, which I learned from Donald Michael Kraig in his book *Modern Magick.* For the most part, these spiritual entities are a form of nonorganized energy, with no intent other than to absorb energy and are, in most cases, harmless. However, there have been certain instances where a person or group of people has attracted the attention of a more powerful entity, which caused many problems for them.

Magical protection should be the first type of magical ritual or spell that you learn. The techniques of protections should be thoroughly understood and utilized if you, as a witch, are going to prosper in your spiritual studies. The witch's bottle, as discussed earlier, is only one method of protection, and it is designed for protection of the individual who makes it, not the home or property where he or she lives. Therefore, one should set up a magical barrier to keep out any negative influences that may be directed toward you. If you are open about your religion in your community, the importance of this type of protection cannot be stressed enough. If your neighbors know that you are a witch, they may be sending negative thought patterns directed toward you. This is something that is not taught by many covens, and it leaves their students open to the ravages of negative energy.

Ritual to Uncross a Home or Business

ITEMS NEEDED

- Purple seven-day candle
- Blue seven-day candle
- ½ cup sea salt
- Pinch of mandrake
- Pinch of basil
- Pinch of ground cloves
- 4oz bottle of Four Thieves vinegar (this is available through most occult suppliers)
- Uncrossing Incense

Combine the sea salt, mandrake, basil, and ground cloves in a small bowl. Place a small portion on the ground in each of the four corners of your property (not the house). If you live in an apartment, wait until nightfall and place at the corners of the building. It is very important that no one sees you doing this in order to prevent any further negative thought patterns to your work or to distract you. Once this is done, take the Four Thieves vinegar and place it into a bowl. Sprinkle it about the house while saying:

> *Vinegar wrought by Thieves of Four;*
> *Send evil out through window and door*
> *Here only peace and love can be;*
> *As I will, so shall it be.*

Burn the incense in the building each day for a week to help remove the negative energy. If possible, open all the doors and windows while the incense is burning; this allows fresh air into the business and helps facilitate the removal of negativity. The purple and blue candles should be burned each day for a week inside the building. The purple candle works to overcome obstacles and the blue candle brings peace to the location.

Ritual to Protect Against Enemies Both Open and Secret

For this spell, you will make use of candle magick as well as the green blood.

ITEMS NEEDED

- 1 Orange Candle
- Protection green blood
- Protection incense
- 1 cup of salt

Once you have made the protection green blood, sprinkle the candle with it using your thumb, index finger, and middle finger of your dominant hand (i.e., the hand you write with). Do not drench the candle so as to wet the wick, but rather dip the fingers in the green blood and flick the moisture onto the candle three times. This attunes the candle to give off protective energies. Sprinkle the salt, using the same three fingers, in a complete circle around the candle and then place the rest of the salt in the green blood mixture. Light the candle and say:

I call upon the elements' power
To protect and turn from me all things sour.
I call on the Spirits of Protection to be with me here
Until the danger is no longer near.
A wall of Protection around me I build,
By magick of candle, spirits, and by my intention willed.
Let no power break this ring which shines around me.
This is my will and so shall it be.

Take up the green blood mixture (now combined with the salt) and go through your home and property, sprinkling it about just as you sprinkled the candle. Just a sprinkle or two per room and at each corner of your property is enough. With the remaining green blood, wash your feet and anoint your forehead and then leave the bowl at the front door of your home until it evaporates. This protection spell will work for quite a while, and needs to be done only once to secure your aura from any negative attack.

A Charm for Protection

This is a general protection charm and is very simple to make.

ITEMS NEEDED

- 1 raw egg

- Red wine
- Rue
- Fennel
- Vervain
- Small vial or container

Pour the red wine into a pot. Add the rue, fennel and vervain to the wine and bring the mixture to a simmer. Once the wine and herbs are heated up, turn off the heat and let it cool.

Hollow out the egg by carefully poking holes at both ends and then blowing out the contents of the egg. You may dispose of the egg any way you choose, but keep the shell. Plug up one end of the eggshell by dripping wax over it. Now, using a small funnel, carefully pour the wine and herb mixture into the eggshell until it is full. Seal the remaining hole with wax and take the egg outside to a large tree, preferably an oak, but if one is not available, any tree will do.

Hold the egg above your head and say:

Within my hand I hold all danger and harm;
Yet I feel no fear or alarm.
For herbs of protection are hid
Inside this container without key or lid.
I hereby destroy all that is harmful to me
And release the protection, so mote it be.

Smash the eggshell against the trunk of the tree so that it shatters. Gather up the pieces of the eggshell and grind them up into a powder. Place this powder into a small vial and wear it on a necklace or carry it with you for protection.

Rite to Remove the Effects of Bad Gossip

Gossip affects us the same way that the evil eye does. It is a projection of negative energy, but this time it is a verbal attack rather than a visual attack. This energy latches onto the aura and hinders good fortune. To remove it, perform the following rite.

ITEMS NEEDED

- 1 cup of Epsom salts
- 1 cup of baking soda
- 2 charcoals
- Frankincense tears
- Censer

This rite begins by taking a spiritual bath with the Epsom salts and baking soda. Combine the two ingredients together and bathe to remove negativity from the aura. When you have completed the bath, light the charcoal and place it in the censer. Open your front door and place the censer on the threshold. Now place some frankincense onto the charcoals and as the smoke rises say the following:

As this incense burns so well,
Those who spread their lies to tell,
Their tongues do burn by this my spell.

Repeat this chant seven times and the spell is done.

CHAPTER 9

DREAMS AND SLEEP

To sleep, perchance to dream . . .

—SHAKESPEARE, *HAMLET*

Dreams have been a fascination of mine since I was a small child. I have vivid memories of my mother and me sitting at the kitchen table discussing over a cup of coffee what we had dreamed in our sleep the previous night. More often than not, we spent many hours trying to figure out just what in the world those dreams could have meant. I suppose that, at the time, my mother had no idea that her curiosity would spread to me and lead me on a trip through the mind and realms of sleep. This was the beginning of my studies into the occult.

Later, when I attended college as a psychology major, I would become enthralled by the ideas of Carl Jung. Finding that my professors, being Behavioral Psychologists, gave little credit to Jung, I made the trek to the campus library and devoured his complete works, something that most of my professors had not even done. Reading into Carl Jung's world, I became even more interested in various techniques of dreams and dream interpretation.

Through my practices using the Tarot, I made many connections between Carl Jung's archetypes and the major arcana of the Tarot. Realizing this, I also made the connection that universal symbols and the collective unconscious are very real and powerful beyond comprehension. These symbols speak to our minds without words and even our conscious understanding. However, they do speak to us, and we do hear, albeit on a subconscious level.

I always stress to those who come to me to learn or to ask me questions regarding any kind of spirituality that dreams are the answers to any problem or question one may have. In ancient Greece, priests who would interpret the dreams of the ill to help discern a cure attended temples of the god Asclepius, god of healing. Learning to decipher the symbols of the dreams is a talent that must be learned and developed by anyone who wishes to become a spiritually minded individual.

THE SCIENCE OF SLEEP

One of the most fascinating aspects of dreaming is the actual sleep process. Sleep is, to science and doctors, just as much a mystery as dreams are. There is actually no theory that fully explains why we sleep. We do know that there is a chemical in the brain that builds up over the course of the day, causing us to become sleepy, and that this chemical is flushed out of the brain while we sleep, but as to the reason why this happens, there is no answer. One theory is that sleep allows the body to relax and build up strength. While this sounds quite reasonable, it just doesn't hold water. When we sleep, our bodies are in constant motion. We roll, twist, turn, jump, and toss. Our bodies actually receive more rest by just sitting still and relaxing while still awake.

Another theory is that we developed sleep during prehistoric times as a defense against animal predators. We would sleep so that our bodies would be still and thus not attract wild animals that might decide we looked rather tasty. Once again, our bodies are not completely still as we sleep. Certainly, a loud snore would likely attract the attention of a hungry animal rather than allow us to be overlooked. Moreover, as we sleep we are totally unconscious and unaware of our surroundings—definitely not a safety mechanism when you are out near wild animals.

In actuality, we have no solid evidence to state why we sleep. My theory is that sleep and dreams are a way for us to reconnect to our divine essence. Whether you call that essence god, goddess, spirit, Akasha, or Od doesn't matter. What does matter is that the connection is there, and it is whatever you make it to be.

While we do not know why we sleep or dream, we do know a great deal about the cycle and process of sleep. Unfortunately, this gives rise to more questions than answers. Follow along with me through the realms of the sleep state.

THE STAGES OF SLEEP

When you enter into your bed at night and close your eyes, your brain immediately begins to emit what are called alpha waves. Alpha waves are the sign that you are mildly relaxed and the mind is beginning to wander. This is the daydream state of mind. Depending on how fast you can relax yourself, within 5 to 10 minutes you will enter into stage one of sleep, which I refer to as the "Gate of Earth." In this stage, your brain begins to give off small, irregular brain wave patterns. Your mind is wandering and considering the affairs of everyday life. This is usually the point where what you are going to dream about takes hold. We all know that our emotions affect our dreams. So if you are thinking about a problem at work when you enter the Gate of Earth, you will more than likely dream something related to your work. Earth is the foundation of everything, thus the Gate of Earth is the foundation of your dreams.

For the most part, we do not consciously decide what we will dream about. The subconscious mind takes care of that for us. However, in advanced stages of dream working, one can learn to program the dream one would like to have. I have had some success with this over the years, but I prefer to hear what my subconscious mind has to tell me.

Stage two of the dream state is called the "Gate of Air." Your brain wave pattern has now become more regular, yet now and again it shows intermittent spikes, or *sleep spindles*. I prefer to think of them as "Blasts of Air." Air is the element of the mind and intellect. In this stage you begin to process the information that will be in your dream. You are, in essence, pondering the dream material. Your subconscious mind is deciding on what symbols it will present to you in order to communicate with your divine essence, or true self.

Stage three is the "Gate of Water." Here you are deeply relaxed and the mind is totally absorbed in the task of sleep. If someone were to try to wake you at this stage, it would take some effort. Your brain wave pattern shows what are called delta waves, confirming the fact that you are completely relaxed. Water is the element of emotion and feelings. Here, the *type* of dream is chosen. Will it be scary, funny, confusing, erotic, senseless, serious, or something else? Here is where the mind sets the stage for the dream and creates the proper atmosphere for the message it wants to convey to you.

Stage four is the "Gate of Fire." Fire is the element of change, action, consumption. Here is where all of the previous elements of the dream are forged and put together to make the dream happen. In this stage you are in a state of deep sleep. If a person is a sleepwalker, this is the stage of sleep he or she is wandering around in, perhaps searching for something. If you have ever seen an actual sleepwalker, you may have been struck with some degree of fear. This is because sleepwalkers are in such a deep state of mind that the energy they give off, the Fire energy, is a powerful force and often quite frightening.

Now here is where the great mystery begins. So far, we have traveled down a fairly straight road. We began with a light, relaxed state and moved gradually down to a deep sleep. This trip has taken roughly 90 minutes; but, so far, we have not reached the dream state. When we have passed the Gate of Fire it would seem logical that we would enter through the "Gate of Dreams," right? Well, we do not. Instead, we work our way back up through the Gates until we reach the Gate of Earth. This happens quickly and without apparent reason.

Once we reach the Gate of Earth we should be in a state of light sleep; however, this also does not happen. Once at the Gate of Earth again, we jump down past all of the Gates into the "Realm of Dreams." This is not a gradual process downward, but an instant change of brain wave patterns.

We have now begun what is called paradoxical sleep. A paradox is something that does not quite make sense, and that is exactly what happens here. The entire skeletal muscular system shuts down completely so that our bodies do not act out the dream that we are having. This sudden muscular shutdown is often the reason why sometimes when we are falling asleep our bodies jerk very hard, startling us awake. Also, at this stage of sleep, the eyes begin to move about under your closed eyelids. This is called REM sleep, or rapid eye movement sleep. When you see REMs, you know the person is dreaming. This whole process may seem odd or unnecessary, until further examination.

Imagine that you built a machine from the ground up and spent much of your time choosing the perfect parts, the right gears, levers, knobs, and lights to do the job you intended the machine to do. Everything you did was the best you could, and the machine was finally finished. Would you immediately plug it in and throw the switch, or would you give it one final look over to make sure you did not forget anything?

Think of it this way: We began our journey at the Gate of Earth where our subconscious mind decided what to dream about. We then moved forward to the Gate of Air where it decided upon the symbols of the dream. Next we passed the Gate of Water to determine what setting the dream would be. Finally we go through the Gate of Fire to put the dream into action. But before the dream actually begins, our mind takes a quick look back over everything it chose at the Gates and makes sure that nothing was left out or forgotten. Then, quite magically, we enter into the Realm of Dreams.

While this may be confusing to the scientific mind, to the witch it is a necessary part of the sleep/dream process. You see, the witch understands that the Law of Cycles applies even to the most minuscule detail. Science can only answer *how* things happen. The witch seeks to know *why*.

Consider the fact that each of us sleeps, on average, eight hours a night. During that eight hours, we enter a dream cycle every ninety minutes. That accounts for roughly five dream cycles per night, each lasting anywhere from fifteen minutes to an hour. That amounts to nearly five hours a night in a pure dream state. Simple multiplication will show that in the course of a year's time you will have spent 1,836.25 hours in the land of dreams! That translates into seventy-six days a year! My point is this: If nature has taught us anything, it is that evolution disposes of whatever does not serve some purpose. So if we spend 20 percent of our time each year in a dream state, it must be pretty important. Right?

Dreams are our tickets to the spiritual worlds that lie beyond the physical senses. Dreams tap into our minds and spirits and allow us direct union with our true selves, without outside interpretation, alteration, or inhibitions to block that truth. I have seen people spend years learning to reach a meditative state in order to find enlightenment, yet each night they ignore the images and visions sent to them by the gods and by their own inner selves. Everything in the universe serves a purpose, and dreams are our easiest route to the path of enlightenment. Never underestimate the dream and never waste the time you spend in your dreams.

A dream is a world in which you are the supreme creator and from which many things can be learned. Of the many thousands of dreams that you will have throughout your life, each of them serves one or more of six purposes.

1. To release the mind from the mundane world
2. To give a symbolic view of our current lives
3. To offer spirit contacts
4. To teach
5. To solve problems in our lives
6. To show us the future

Each of us dreams approximately 1,500 dreams per year. That translates to about 90,000 dreams that you will have dreamed by the time you are sixty years old. Where does all this dream material come from? Well, all dreams emanate from activity in our brains, but when you dream, the actual information presented to you comes from one or more of the following seven sources:

1. The collective unconscious
2. A past life
3. Various spirits or entities
4. Genetic memory of your immediate family or ancestors

5. The time you spent in the womb before birth
6. Your childhood or earlier adulthood
7. Your present and current life

To confuse matters even more, sometimes dreams can combine two or three, sometimes more, of these sources together in a single dream. Then it is up to you to decide where everything is coming from—and of course, why.

There are ten distinct types of dreams that most of us experience throughout our lives.

1. *Physiological dreams* - These dreams often depict such bodily functions as having sex, feeling aches and pains, urinating, pregnancy, and so on.

2. *Vigilant dreams* - These are dreams that often contain images that directly involve changes in the environment of the room. For example, you are asleep and the phone rings. In your dream you hear a phone ringing and you answer it. The actual waking world affected your dream.

3. *Problem-solving dreams* - These dreams present a symbolic solution to a problem. They often occur during times of confusion or stress. Thinking of the problem at hand before sleep then triggers the mind, and the solution comes in the form of a dream. There is a story that the inventor of the sewing machine, when trying to figure out a way to get the machine to push the needle through and back again, fell asleep at his work area. In his dream, he was running from a tribe of headhunters, who were throwing spears at him. The spears were long and thin and had a hole in them near the tip. When he awoke from the dream, he realized that if he used a needle with the hole placed near the tip rather than at the end, his machine would work. Thus, the spears in the dream were the answer to his problem.

4. *Residual dreams* - These are dreams that contain the events of the day you just had. They may be dreams of work, home, yard chores, and such.

5. *Contrary dreams* - These are dreams that present the opposite of the feeling that prevailed at the time of sleep. During periods of great depression, sometimes we dream of laughter and joy, and vice versa. These dreams are designed to bring about emotional or spiritual balance.

6. *Transforming dreams* - In these dreams, you perform some magical act that completely transforms a situation or object into what you want it to be. For example, you may be dreaming about being chased, and then suddenly you turn and face your assailant and command him to stop chasing you. The assailant stops and disappears from the dream. You have changed the course of the dream and, in essence, changed fear into courage within your own mind and self.

7. *Wish-fulfilling dreams* - These are dreams in which your wishes are made manifest, i.e., making love to your favorite movie star, winning the lottery, finding lots of money on the street. Although these dreams are designed to give you pleasure and excitement, they also keep you from becoming consciously obsessed with things in the material world. You "live out" the fantasy in the dream; thus it does not affect you as much when you awake.

8. *Recurrent dreams* – In these dreams, the same images recur over the span of several nights; sometimes they can continue throughout a person's entire life. These dreams are of the utmost importance to the dreamer and must be interpreted so that the message is clear. A dream of falling from a high place is a common recurring dream.

9. *Nightmares* - These are dreams in which frightening and hor-

rific images appear. These dreams often affect people even after waking and are presented to instill courage. When having a nightmare, you must turn it into a transforming dream by conquering the horrific image. These terrible images are often symbolic representations of a problem that you are facing in the waking world.

10. *Insight dreams* - These are dreams in which images that are new or unknown to the dreamer present themselves in a profound way or merely symbolically. An example of this type of dream would be dreaming that a certain formula will cure an illness and then applying that same formula in the waking world to find that it does indeed work.

HOW TO CHARGE AND
USE A MAGICAL DREAM STONE

Timing: This ritual can be done during the full moon, preferably when she is occupying a water sign (Cancer, Pisces, Scorpio). However, for the best results, you should perform this ritual during your peak astrological dreamtime. To find this time you will need a natal birth chart. Beginning with your sun sign, you count counterclockwise nine signs. See what sign occupies this house. When the moon enters this sign, this is your peak dreamtime. Performing this ritual for charging your dream stone during this peak time will give the most powerful results.

Location: Preferably Outdoors.

Setup: Sacred Space

ITEMS NEEDED:

• Mugwort infusion

- Moonstone
- Salt
- Vessel of pure water
- 3 seven-day candles (black, gray, and blue)
- Your athame (See Concerning the Athame, chapter 6.)

Begin by mentally drawing a circle about you with your Athame (If you don't have a ritual knife, use the index finger of your dominant hand). Take three pinches of salt and add it to the vessel of pure water. Stir the water and salt together in a clockwise motion; then sprinkle the water about the circle, starting from the north, and say the following:

In the name of the Great Mother and Father God
And by the Ancient Spirits of the land
I cleanse this circle and charge it with the
powers of Good Fortune.
By the might of Moon and Sun
In the name of Magick be it done.

The circle you have just mentally drawn about yourself is now considered Sacred Space. Within Sacred Space, you can do anything that you would normally do in a ritually cast circle, except raise power. Raising power is normally done through chanting and dancing within a ritually cast circle. The circle, in witchcraft, is used to hold the raised energy in so that it builds up tremendous strength. Then that energy can be released at just the right moment to go out and affect a change in reality.

Take your jar of mugwort infusion and place the moonstone inside it, then set it on the ground. Arrange your three candles in a downward pointing triangle around the jar. Beginning at the upper left corner of the triangle, light the candle and say:

One light for Nyx, Goddess of the Realm of Night.

Move to the right corner of the triangle and light that candle saying:

One light for Somnus, God of the Realm of Sleep.

Move now downward and light the last candle and say:

One light for Morpheus, God of the Realm of Dreams.

Visualize a beam of black light coming from the Nyx candle and entering into the jar and infusing the mugwort infusion and moonstone with power. From the Somnus candle comes a gray beam of light, and from the Morpheus candle comes a blue beam of light. The three beams meet within the glass jar and infuse the stone and liquid with the powers of Night, Sleep, and Dreams.

Visualize now the jar glowing with the silver light of the moon. Hold this image for as long as you can. When the image fades, move everything indoors and allow the candles to burn out on their own. When the candles are out, take the moonstone out of the mugwort infusion and allow it to air dry. Place the stone into a black bag and never let it be exposed to sunlight or electric lights but only to candlelight or moonlight. The mugwort infusion can be discarded by pouring it out at the base of a tree.

To use the dream stone, place it under your pillow when you go to bed; you are sure to have incredible dreams. Results will vary from person to person, depending on how good your visualization skills are. The stone should be recharged from time to time. To do this, simply hold it to the full moon and visualize it glowing with moonlight.

HOW TO MAKE AND USE
A TEA TO ENHANCE YOUR DREAMS

If you find that dream recall is very difficult or if you feel that you are not even dreaming, I have a possible solution for you. The following tea is sacred to the god Morpheus, ruler of the dream world.

Purchase a small amount of balm of Gilead herb and anise seeds. With your mortar and pestle, break the balm of Gilead pods open. (Remember, you should have two separate mortars: one for toxic herbs and one for edible herbs. Use the mortar for edible herbs for this operation.) It is not necessary to grind them, just crack them open. Use two tablespoons of crushed pods and one teaspoon of anise seed. Place them in your coffee filter and brew it like you would a pot of coffee. Drink one or two cups of the tea prior to sleep.

I have used this tea on many occasions and have suggested its use to dozens of people, and nearly everyone has raved of its abilities to open psychic channels and especially enhance the dream cycle. On the numerous occasions that I have used the tea, I have noticed that the only side effect of the tea is that the following morning it leaves me in a very lazy mood, and occasionally it seems to have caused a slight swelling in my tonsils. I have asked others who have tried the tea about these side effects, and they have said they had no such experiences.

However, one woman, a coworker of mine, had tried the tea to help her relax, as she was having trouble sleeping due to pains in her sides. At the time she had no idea that she suffered from huge gallstones. The tea acted as a healing agent, seeking out the stones and loosening them from her gallbladder. Unfortunately, they were too large to be passed, and she was forced to have surgery. She is now fine and swears by the healing properties of this tea.

So, as a word of warning, if you believe that you suffer from any kind of kidney or gallstones do not take this tea before consulting a doctor. If you feel uncertain about taking the tea, be on the safe side and take only one cup of the tea at first, to be certain of no side effects. In any case, I'm sure you will find the tea most delightful to drink and quite amazing in its effects.

The dreams that are opened by this tea are often erratic and make little sense. However, they are extremely vivid and colorful. I have had instances where people who have never recalled dreaming in color drank this tea and awoke in astonishment at the array of rainbow-like landscapes and people in their dreams. Some have even spoken of the dreams lasting throughout the night and continuing the following night.

I am most curious to hear any stories related to the use of this tea to help in dreaming, so if you try it (and I highly recommend that you do) please write me and let me know of the results.

CHAPTER 10

DIVINATION: CONSULTING THE DEITIES

As they say of the priestess at Delphi, when she drinks of the second fountain, that she is immediately full of the god, and delivers her oracle to all who ask for it.

—LUCIAN, GREEK SATIRIST

Divination is the art of discovering what is unknown by the use of various techniques designed to contact a person's inner divinity/spirit or to make direct contact with a person's outer deity or deities. For the use of divination associated with the practices discussed in this book, contact with the outer deities is what will be discussed.

Technically, anything that consults a particular deity is considered an oracle more than a divination and is much more accurate, although more obscure. In ancient Greece, oracles were sanctioned by the government and were consulted by persons from all over the known world of the time. The Oracle of Delphi was probably the most celebrated oracle.

Answers given by the ancient oracles were often two sided, and it was up to the individual to determine what the oracle meant. In the end, however, the oracle was always correct. For example, the

Spartans, upon consulting an oracle and asking about their war with the Arcadians, were told: "You will dance on conquered land, and piece it out among yourselves." The Spartans took this as a sure sign of their victory, but they failed to see the true meaning of the Oracle. The Spartans did indeed dance on conquered land, but it was their own conquered land, and under bondage.

An oracle is your direct contact to the gods and goddesses. Use it regularly and use it wisely. No important work should be undertaken without first convening with the deities. Remember, the choice is yours as to whether or not you follow the advice of the divination or oracle.

Consulting the deities and divination should be an integral part of every witch's life, as should prayer. Once a week, upon waking, go before your shrine and pray a prayer of devotion to your deities, ask for guidance and perform a divination to bring about balance. This can also be done to find imbalances in others. Consulting the deities for balance and guidance need only be performed once a week; after all, if you are following the tenets, there should be little that will affect you adversely. The consultation should be focused on what is out of balance in your life for that time or for that week. As every witch knows, balance is the key to happiness and success. By discovering what is out of balance in our lives, we know what must be done to bring us back into alignment with the world around us.

WITCH'S COIN DIVINATION

This is a technique of oracular divination that can be used to attain an answer as to what is out of balance in your life. For this divination technique, you will need four coins. Any type coin will do, or even four small, wooden disks. Paint one side of the coin white, the other side black. This system of divining events is similar to the Chinese I-Ching, but only sixteen patterns can arise, which makes it also very

similar to the Arabic geomantic divinations. It acts doubly as a divination as well as an oracle upon which the gods and goddesses can
send direct messages to you.

Upon waking in the morning, approach your shrine and say your
morning prayers. Take up the coins and pray for guidance as you shuffle the coins back and forth in your hands. When you feel that the
time is right, lightly flip your hand, with all four coins in it, down
upon the altar, keeping your hand over the coins so that they do not
scatter about. Now, look at the coins and observe the pattern that
arises from top to bottom. The coin furthest from you is the top, and
the one closest is the bottom. Consult the following interpretations
for your answer.

Air of Air - When this pattern falls, it symbolizes a steady moving
   ○   wind. Things will move along at a steady, comfortable pace.
   ○   You are in balance, and no spiritual work is necessary; how-
   ○   ever, with good fortune on your side it is important to
   ○   remember the tenet of humility. Do not let your good stand-
        ing bring arrogance or conceit.

Fire of Air - This pattern symbolizes violent wind. Things are erratic
   ○   and moving too swiftly for you to keep up. Avoid all forms of
   ○   conflict, as anger and violence are associated with this pat-
   ○   tern. You need to perform an uncrossing ritual combined
   ●   with a cleansing bath for seven days. Perform the bath for
        three days; then perform the uncrossing ritual given in this
        book. This pattern also symbolizes meeting a new person.

Earth of Air - This pattern shows a soft breeze that does not knock
   ○   objects down, simply goes around them. Flexibility is the key
   ○   word to keep in mind here. You must be flexible in all walks
   ●   of life. You are in balance, but do not fully understand the
   ●   spiritual forces that have put you in balance. You are simply

floating in the winds, so to say. Meditate daily on the four elements of nature.

Water of Fire - This is symbolized by a reflection of fire upon the face of the water. The reflection of the fire can be seen, and the water can be felt, but neither can be put together in actuality without one destroying the other. This means that your life is at a standstill. There is no action, no movement, no advancement. This is caused by feelings of jealousy, greed, and/or anger. To counteract this pattern's effect, begin a new project and remember the creed of perfect love and perfect trust.

Earth of Earth - This pattern speaks of solidity and receptivity. When this pattern falls, you are completely out of balance and moving away from your destiny. Although things may seem fine, you are not living up to your potential. The predominance of earth energy has caused you to become stagnant. Conflict and strife will result, as spirit tries to bring you back on your destiny's path. Perform the rite to protect you from both open and secret enemies and bathe in a water herb bath for seven days.

Air of Water - This is represented by evaporating water. You understand that water is evaporating, but you cannot actually see it. This pattern tells that someone close to you is betraying you behind your back. You feel that this is true, but cannot tell who it is or why the person is doing it. This negativity aimed toward you can lead to physical illness. Perform healing rituals and take purification baths for three days.

Fire of Water - This signifies violent or boiling water. You are at total conflict with yourself and with others. Do work to overcome enemies both hidden and open. Take a spiritual hex-breaking bath and then take a benzoin resin "smoke bath" (see The Smoke Bath, chapter 8) to eliminate problems with others.

Air of Earth - Symbolized by level ground and open plains. You are
●   balanced, but jealousy from others can bring you quickly out
●   of balance. Perform the ritual to send back evil and make a
○   charm to protect you from the evil eye. Wear this charm for
○   one moon cycle.

Water of Water - This is signified by stagnant water. Water that does not
●   move becomes stale and murky. Things are not moving as you
○   would like, but you must avoid the temptation to use magick
●   in an unethical way to get things going. Do not feel guilt for
○   mistakes you have made in the past; simply do not make them
again now. Perform purification baths to remove "bad" energy
and perform a rite designed to "open new roads."

Fire of Fire - This is the pattern of violent fire. Things are moving very
○   fast for you now. It is almost overwhelming. The sudden
●   influx of energy has caused you to become at odds with your-
○   self. You are causing your own bad luck with negative thought
●   patterns. Perform rituals and cleansings to overcome self-
deception and self-hexing.

Water of Earth - This is the Life-giving earth and symbolizes return. As
●   we know, the earth gives rise to all life, yet all life on Earth is
●   not of a positive nature. This pattern speaks that another may
●   be working negative magick against you. It can also represent
○   that your bad-luck is the result of the three-fold law return-
ing on you. Perform rituals to protect yourself from enemies
and do work to change bad luck into good luck.

Earth of Fire - This is signified by the great crevices created during
○   earthquakes. This pattern shows that others are jealous of
●   your accomplishments and are gossiping about you in a neg-
●   ative way. Keep your tenet of humility and do not let success
●   go to your head. Stand up for the truth and do work to protect yourself from the effects of bad gossip.

Earth of Water - This pattern can be demonstrated by splashing water
● onto a wall. The water will cling and stick to the wall, slowly
○ dripping off or evaporating, but not before it totally wets
● whatever it touches. Negativity is running rampant in your
● life now. Perform both spiritual and physical cleansings on
yourself and your home and property. Perform a protection
rite for your home to keep all evil out. If you do not have a
witch's bottle, construct one.

Fire of Earth - This is violent earth. Volcanic eruptions are the best
● analogy for this type of energy. Watch your words—and your
● back. Keep a heavy tongue when speaking of your affairs or
○ ideas. Others do not wish to see you succeed with your plans.
● Remember, a witch must know, dare, will, and *keep silent!*
Create a protection charm and wear for one full moon cycle.

Air of Fire - This is symbolized by the perpetual, never ending fire.
○ This pattern tells that another person is working negative
● magick against you—most probably a love spell. Do work to
○ uncross yourself. Meditation on your patron deity will bring
○ further insight into the problem at hand.

Water of Air - This pattern speaks of modesty and symbolizes a closed
○ chamber, where air becomes stale. You are out of balance due to
○ the demands of daily life. Work, school, or love life have preoc-
● cupied your time and pulled you away from spirituality. Offerings
○ to the deities and to your familiar spirit will bring balance back
into your life. Perform work to increase your self-confidence.

CONCERNING WHETHER
TO WORK MAGICK FOR OTHERS

I mentioned earlier that very few witches open their abilities up to the
public. This may seem odd to some of you reading this, because most

books on the subject of witchcraft and magick say that you should not perform magick for others. Other books may say that magick can only be performed for those who have given you permission to do so. In this way, you will bypass any negative repercussions that may result from the spell.

The logic behind this thought is that if you perform spells on others or for others without their knowledge or permission, then you are manipulating their lives to suit your will. While this may be true, sometimes magick must remain secret, and therefore the people cannot know that you are working for them. This is a tricky situation. How do you determine when and how to perform magick for others? Once again, divination is the key.

Perform a divination to see if you are allowed to help your client magically. If the divination says yes, then you begin to find out what type of work is to be done. If the divination says, no, then you tell the person what he or she must do. I have been practicing and using my craft for the public for quite a while and I have used this technique with absolutely no negative side effects to speak of.

The best method to use when performing magick for others is to first, of course, find out if you are allowed to intervene. This can be done using the coin oracle. Take up the coins and shake them back and forth in your hands and then flip them down as described earlier in the Witch's Coin Divination. Look at the pattern and consult the following chart to determine the answer:

1. Light - This pattern shows all four coins with the white sides up. This is a pattern that gives a yes answer with a blessing on the work from the gods.

2. Conflict - This pattern is any combination showing three white and one black coin. This pattern tells that there will be struggles to achieve the goal at hand. It would be best to not get involved.

3. Balance - This pattern is any combination showing two black coins and two white coins. This pattern gives a definite yes answer, showing that the desired result would bring balance to all people involved.
4. Confusion- This pattern shows three black coins and one white in any combination. This pattern tells that there is too much confusion surrounding the situation and it would be best to not get involved until things become a little clearer.
5. Darkness - This pattern is four black coins and always gives a no answer. The desired result is against the destiny of those involved, and to work magick would bring only negative outcomes.

Once you have determined whether you can perform magick for the purpose, you should instruct the client to take a series of spiritual baths that will attune his or her energies to those that you will be working with. The next thing you determine is which deities would be most beneficial to work with for the client. For example, if the client lacks love, you might want to try working with Aphrodite or Eros. Once you determine the deity, you then perform an offertory rite, asking the deity to bless the work you are performing and aid in its effects. The third thing to do is to perform the actual spell work. This can be anything from candle burning, to a charm bag, to a charged water spell, anything and anyway that you feel the magick should be sent.

CHAPTER 11

GODS, GODDESSES, AND OTHER SPIRITS

True philosophy is to simply love the gods in both your thoughts and heart, and to follow their goodness without the intrusion of pointless opinions.

—MONTE PLAISANCE

No doubt the most consistent aspect of Wicca among the various groups or traditions is the concept of two deities or gods. These are often viewed as a god and a goddess. It is a common belief among witches, and one that is hard to argue with, that there can be no creation without both male and female. The male is the energy that sets things into motion, while the female is the energy that nurtures that motion and brings it to life. Just as in the act of conception, it is the man who activates the process, while the woman is left to give birth and nurture.

Now, there can be some argument over whose role is more important (or painful), but one cannot argue that both roles are not necessary for the act of creation to take place. Therefore, it is illogical to the witch to believe in a male deity or god as the one true god. To the witch, all gods and goddesses are simply different views of the lord and lady. Polarity is the key. The individual witch must choose which god and goddess he or she feels most in tune with.

To put this into simpler terms, think of it in this way. Electricity is an energy that we all are familiar with. But in my state, the electric company is called LP&L, and in your state the electric company is called CP&L. Is your electricity the One True Electricity? Is my electricity any better than yours? The energy is the same, it's just that it is a lot easier for me to deal with LP&L than with CP&L. Likewise, as a witch, I choose the energy sources (deities) that are easier for me to deal with as well as those energies (deities) that are closer to home. This is why many witches research their historical roots, in order to determine the pantheon that they are most in tune with. A witch with an ancestry in Germany, may choose Odin and Freya as their lord and lady, while a witch with Celtic ancestry may choose Cernunnos and Cerridwen. The important thing to remember is that there is not a One True God or Goddess. All deities should be treated with the respect and honor that they deserve.

Concerning Patron Deities

The patron deity causes much confusion for beginning students. I have often heard students tell me that they would rather not choose only one or two deities with which to work, as this would limit their outlook. This is an understandable point, but it lacks a true under-standing of what the patron deities are all about.

Think about it as though you were living in ancient Greece. You might be a priest or priestess of Aphrodite. Would this mean that you could not believe in any of the other deities of Mount Olympus? No. You would understand and acknowledge all deities. You would even pray to other deities, but you would have particular deities with whom you felt the most affinity.

While we are on the subject of deities, I feel that I must dispel a common misconception that has become quite popular amid many neopagan groups. This misconception attempts to reduce the deities of all religions to mere projections of the mind. In essence, they are saying that the existence of all gods and goddesses of all ancient and modern cultures stems from and depends on a human conception of them.

This is a false and dangerous attitude to take. The gods exist! That is as plain and simple as I can put it. Did they exist prior to human belief in them? That, I am afraid, we will never know, for the obvious reason that we were not here.

Let me say this, however, to try to clear this up a little more. When humans were just beginning, they looked upon the stars, lightning, wind, and oceans with awe and respect. What caused the wind to blow? Where did lightning come from? Obviously there were forces at work that they could not understand and that were far more powerful than they were. So in order to understand these forces better, they gave them names and made them as people. Thus, Zeus was a god of thunder and lightning; Thetis, the goddess of the sea, and so on. All aspects of life that could not be explained were given a form that they could understand. Therefore, although the gods may not have existed in name and form, the power that they represent has always been with us and will continue to exist as long as nature endures. So just because there was not a god named Zeus from the beginning of recorded history, doesn't mean that his lightning bolts did not light up the sky and thunder roll across the plains.

Choosing a Patron Deity

To those of you that I have taken as my children, I shall be as thy mother, taking care of your needs in return for your loyalty and devotion to me.

—As spoken to Lord Corvus of Thessaly by the
Goddess Hekate (1998)

Choosing a patron deity should be a carefully considered process. In the beginning, the patrons should be deities who are endowed with abilities that you are trying to acquire. If you cannot actually choose a deity, you must consult the oracle to determine which deities are willing to work with you.

I always recommend that you choose a male and female deity with whom to work. Do not fall into the trap that your god and goddess must be lovers. This does not have to be. These deities whom you are choosing are for your personal advancement in the studies of witchcraft. They are an energy source that you are tapping into and that you can use to bring yourself closer to divinity.

The only restriction that you should have when choosing patron deities is that they should be from the same pantheon. Do not mix pantheons, as this will bring confusion. The energy of a Greek deity does not mix well with the energy of, say, a Norse deity. Now, there are cases where this is not true. The Celtic deity Cernunnos seems to blend well into just about any pantheon. Also, many ancient civilizations did indeed blend their deities with those of foreign countries. The Greeks and Egyptians are a good example of this blending of pantheons. But for the beginning, stick to the same pantheon.

Using the Coin Oracle to Determine Your Patron Deities

It is often said that a witch does not choose their patron deity, but rather, the deity chooses the witch. So, for this operation of the oracle, you will ask which deity wishes to work with you on a personal basis, and it will require the assistance of another witch or friend. The deity who wishes to have you as his or her priest or priestess must answer through the oracle.

This process is quite simple and renders very good results when performed properly. Take up two stones, one white and one black, and shuffle them back and forth in your hands. While doing this, ask for the patron gods or goddesses of your pantheon to speak through the coins and reveal their presence to you. Separate the stones—one in each hand—and hold your closed hands out to your sides. Have your assistant take up the four coins, shake them, and toss them down (see Witch's Coin Divination in chapter 10). Consult the following chart to see which hand should be opened.

Select the right hand for:
Water of Fire
Earth of Earth
Fire of Air
Earth of Air
Air of Air
Water of Water
Fire of Water
Earth of Fire

Select left hand for:
Earth of Water
Fire of Earth
Air of Fire
Water of Air
Air of Earth
Air of Water
Fire of Fire
Water of Fire

When you have determined which hand to open, do so. If the white stone is in that hand, then your patron has spoken and it is their pattern that lies on the table or ground before you. Consult the list below to see who it is. (NOTE: I give the Greek deities in this example because that is the pantheon within which I work. See the charts following it for deities from various other pantheons and their corresponding patterns.) If the stone is the black one, then you must shuffle the stones again and pray for your patron to speak. Throw the coins again and see which hand to open. Do this until you get the white stone. It can take some time, but the results are worth the effort.

Pattern	God	Goddess
Air of Air	Zeus	Athena
Earth of Earth	Hades	Selene
Fire of Water	Eros	Hera
Water of Fire	Kronos	Demeter
Earth of Air	Chiron	Tyche
Air of Earth	Poseidon	Thetis
Earth of Fire	Dionysus	Aphrodite
Water of Earth	Morpheus	Nemysis
Fire of Air	Thanatos	Persephone
Air of Water	Helios	Hekate
Earth of Water	Pan	Nyx
Fire of Earth	Apollo	Hebe
Air of Fire	Hermes	Hestia
Water of Air	Aries	Artemis
Fire of Fire	Horkos	Dike
Water of Water	Hephaestos	Gaea

DEITIES ASSOCIATED WITH THE COIN PATTERNS

Below are listed the coin patterns that are given to the various deities of different pantheons. I have compiled this information as best I can. There are many similarities between the pantheons of the gods and goddesses of different cultures, but there are also many differences. Some of these patterns may have the same deities, and some may have deities you have never heard of. My tradition lies in the Greco-Roman pantheon, and it is with these deities that I have the closest understanding. Thus I was able to fine-tune the deity associations through my experiences with these deities.

These patterns come from a blending of research and some experiences with the deities named. However, these patterns are by no means written in stone, and should you feel, by experience, that a particular deity is more in tune with a different pattern than the one I have listed, feel free to change it. The reader should always remember the Law of Challenge. If something below makes little sense to you, question it and find the truest meaning for yourself through knowledge and experience. Blessed be.

Air of Air
Celtic - Cerridwen
Roman - Diana
Etruscan - None
Babylonian - Nannar
Egyptian - Khonsu

Earth of Earth
Celtic - Cernunnos
Roman - Dianus
Etruscan - Tivs
Babylonian - Sin
Egyptian - Ta-Urt

Fire of Water
Celtic - The Dagda
Roman - Mercurius
Etruscan - Turms
Babylonian - Nabu
Egyptian - Thoth

Water of Fire
Celtic - The Morrigan
Roman - Saturn
Etruscan - Uni
Babylonian - Ishtar
Egyptian - Ptah

Earth of Air
Celtic - Brighid
Roman - Sol
Etruscan - Catha
Babylonian - Shamash
Egyptian - Ra

Air of Earth
Celtic - Lugh
Roman - Nomius
Etruscan - Hercle
Babylonian - Shamash
Egyptian - Amun-Ra

Earth of Fire
Celtic - Rhiannon
Roman - Minerva
Etruscan - Tinia

Water of Earth
Celtic - Diancecht
Roman - Juno
Etruscan - Tagni

Babylonian - Marduk
Egyptian - Maat

Babylonian - Ea
Egyptian - Net

Fire of Air
Celtic - Llyr
Roman - Kore
Etruscan - Tinia
Babylonian - Adad
Egyptian - Hapi

Air of Water
Celtic - Macha
Roman - Janus
Etruscan - Tana
Babylonian - Ninurta
Egyptian - Horus of Edfu

Earth of Water
Celtic - Scathach
Roman - Mars
Etruscan - Maris
Babylonian - Nusku
Egyptian - Sekhmet

Fire of Earth
Celtic - Branwen
Roman - Mercurius
Etruscan - Cilans
Babylonian - Nabu
Egyptian - Thoth

Air of Fire
Celtic - Angus mac Og
Roman - Venus
Etruscan - Turan
Babylonian - Ishtar
Egyptian - Bast

Water of Air
Celtic - Pwyll
Roman - Volcanus
Etruscan - Sethlans
Babylonian - Nusku
Egyptian - Heru-Behutet

Fire of Fire
Celtic - Blodeuwedd
Roman - Venus
Etruscan - Turan
Babylonian - Ishtar
Egyptian - Hathor

Water of Water
Celtic - Sucellus
Roman - Zeus
Etruscan - Minerva
Babylonian - Adad
Egyptian - Amun-Ra

CONCERNING OFFERINGS AND SACRIFICES

In modern witchcraft, the word *sacrifice* is, for the most part, strictly taboo. The more appropriate term is *offering*. For many people, the word sacrifice immediately brings to mind the idea of "animal sacrifice," but this is simply not the essence of what sacrifice is about.

To sacrifice is "to give up." In the case of animal sacrifices, the ancients were offering up the spirit of the sacrificial animal to the deity or deities. In this way, they were "feeding" the deity with energy so that the connection would become stronger between the worshiper and the divine being. This takes place because blood is the most powerful of magical agents, or, as they are called in occult circles, fluid condensers. Some modern religious practices, such as Santeria and even Judaism, still use animal sacrifice in worship and for magical practices. Having witnessed one of these rites first hand, I can safely say that the energy is indeed powerful. However, these practices are not necessary to connect with a deity or to effectively cast a spell, and they are generally frowned upon by mainstream Wicca.

For the witch, sacrifice comes in one of two forms. The first being that of self-sacrifice and the second that of offerings. Let us look at these two subjects more closely.

Self-sacrifice simply means the giving up of something that you hold dear, or cherish, to the deity in exchange for a stronger connection. For example, you have a bracelet that, although it is not worth much monetarily, means a great deal to you. You could offer up that to the lord and lady as a sign of devotion. I am not saying to give up all that you own and live the life of a pauper so that you can connect with a deity. Simple things are all the lord and lady require.

Self-sacrifice also encompasses the giving of time and effort to accomplish something in the name of the god and goddess. For example, you could give up one hour of TV time to sit in prayer and meditation upon your goddess and god. This would be a wonderful sacrifice and would serve to strengthen your connection with your patron deities.

Offerings are the second type of sacrifice given by witches, and probably the most common. An offering is the leaving of certain objects that are sacred to the particular deity. Offerings are made in order to honor a deity or to petition the deity to see things in your favor. This is very important, as there are times when magick should not be used to effect change, but prayer to a deity is acceptable. This allows the deity to take care of things as is best for all involved. There are many different types of offerings that can be given, and the way in which these offerings are given can be complex.

Burnt Offerings

These are offerings that are burned in a fire that is set on the altar. Naturally, these offerings would only consist of flammable objects such as incense, plants, wood from a sacred tree, or food. Burnt offerings are given to deities of the Upper World and to spirits of the Air and Fire. These offerings are made on outdoor altars erected solely for this purpose. When the object is placed in the fire, the following words are to be said:

As this offering is consumed by the flames, let all that hinders my success in (purpose for giving the offering) *be consumed and destroyed, leaving only open roads and clear skies for my journey to success.*

When the prayers are being spoken, it is most important that your hands be placed upon the altar. This is a time-honored and ancient custom that I have found to be crucial to the success of offerings given up at the altar. In ancient times it was said that:

Those that in these words pray, and altar touch,
The omnipotent doth hear.

Placed Offerings

These are offerings that are deliberately left in a place that is considered sacred to the deity in order that the deity or spirit might descend and consume the energy of the offering. In this way the deity and the connection between you and the deity is strengthened.

Food offerings are the most common type of placed offering. Do not scatter the food about on the ground when leaving a placed offering, but rather fix a nice plate, just as you would for any guest eating at your table. Then go out and leave the offering in a special place or simply leave it before a statue of the deity in your household shrine. These types of offerings are most often given to fairies, woodland gods and goddesses and any other type of Middle World deity or spirit.

Buried Offerings

These are most often given to Underworld deities and can consist of any object, be it food, wine, water, or an inanimate object. The only difference is that the offering is buried in the ground or placed within an Underworld entrance such as a cave, a hollowed tree stump, or perhaps the base of a tree where erosion may have exposed the roots. This allows the Underworld deities or spirits to acquire the offering much more easily.

THE DEITIES AND THEIR OFFERINGS

Now that we have discussed the technicalities behind offerings and how they are to be made, let us discuss what types of offerings are most appropriate. Below is a list of offerings appropriate to the type of deity or spirit you may be working with.

Upper World Deities:

Food Offerings. Foods that are white in color, such as bread, white wine, ambrosia (wine, honey, and cream mixed in equal proportions), and various types of fruit nectars.

Objects. Wood from sacred trees, a special incense blend created for that specific deity, objects that are white in color: pearls, quartz crystals, silver coins, etc. Sculptured animals that are sacred to that deity.

Middle World Deities:

Food Offerings. These deities like offerings of cooked food. Usually no special kind of food is necessary. Whatever food is common to your household is fine,but if you are taking from the same pot that you are eating from, make certain that you give the first helping to the deity. This is common courtesy.

Objects. Middle world deities love trinkets. Anything like a bracelet, necklace, ring, or something of that nature can be used. If you are a hunter, many woodland deities like to have the first meat from a kill. This is to be left on a small altar in the woods.

Underworld Deities:

Food Offerings. Ambrosia, pomegranates, fava beans, eggs, and meats of any kind. Bread is also a good offering to Underworld deities. Research into a particular deity will also reveal what foods are favored, and these too can be offered.

Objects. A fire of sacred wood burned in a pit, incense, black stones, coins, flowers, or any object that might be associated with that particular deity. Coins are especially associated with Underworld deities because of the ancient Greek custom of burying the dead with coins in the mouth. This was to pay the ferryman, Charon, for passage across the river Styx.

How to Determine If the Deity Has Accepted an Offering or Sacrifice

Once you have prepared your offering or sacrifice and have left it or offered it up in the proper way, there is still the matter of determining if the deity has accepted it. Sometimes your petition may not reach the deity because you were not sincere enough in your prayers or petitions, or perhaps the offering was ignored or avoided because you asked the deity for something that that deity was not willing to help you with at the time.

To determine if a deity has accepted an offering, it is necessary for you to have an observant eye. The easiest determination is for a food offering you have left on your household shrine. To determine if it is accepted, you need only go back and inspect the offering. An accepted offering will have dried and shrunk slightly in size. This is especially true of bread and fruits. If the offering has begun to rot, then the deity has not accepted it and you must consult the oracle to determine why.

For the other types of offerings, it is a good idea that after the offering is placed, you ask the deity for a sign of acceptance. To do this, simply state aloud:

> *If this, my petition, thou dost hear,*
> *Then in three days time grant me a token of proof.*
> *Let me hear the call of bird, the bark of a dog, or the neigh of*
> *a horse.*

Of course, the sign can be anything, but be specific in what you want to see and when you want to see it. The traditional time is within three days, and the sign usually takes the form of an animal or natural event.

When I first petitioned the goddess Hekate to be my patron, I asked for the sign of a black bird's call. The following day I stepped out of my house to go visit a friend down the street. Atop a telephone pole, I saw a black bird that called out. As I walked I wondered if that was my sign. I visited my friend and started back home, still wondering if the black bird on the pole was my sign from the goddess. As I rounded the turn into my driveway I was stopped in my tracks by a loud shriek. There on the fence was an enormous black bird only two to three feet away from me. It looked me directly in the eyes and cawed aloud. Then it spread its wings and, with what seemed to be a nod of its head, flew away. I stood there in the driveway for several minutes before I found enough strength to walk into the house.

I also have a close friend who asked the goddess Diana for a sign of her existence. Shortly after asking for this sign, he got into his car and drove to a store. The entire way there and back he saw nearly a dozen owls, sacred to the goddess, swooping in front of his car. He had not seen one owl near his home since he was a child, let alone nearly a dozen. Needless to say, he became a true believer. I tell you these stories so that you can see and understand what the signs can appear as and to let you know what to expect when you ask the gods and goddesses for something.

CONCERNING THE WATCHERS

The Watchers are a race of spiritual beings who have been associated with magick and specifically witchcraft since time began. A promise was made long ago to those who practiced the craft that if the

Watchers were remembered and called upon at every gathering, they would lend extra power to our work, and they would witness our rites. By witnessing, the Watchers acknowledge and protect those who are in the craft. In addition to the god and goddess, the Watchers are our spiritual caretakers and guides, both in life and in death.

Although the Watchers are associated with specific directions within the circle, they are not rulers of the elements, as is often believed. In ancient Greece, they were viewed as the Four Winds. Even in the cabalistic orders they are viewed as the archangels. The Watchers are actually stellar beings, each associated with a specific star in the sky. It is said that the many stars are actually campfires of the Watcher's armies.

Very little is written about these Watchers, and in my efforts to fully understand these entities, I performed a series of invocations and evocations for each of the Watchers. Below is the information that I received both from research and from contact with these entities.

The names for the Watchers will vary from tradition to tradition, and to rule out any preconceptions that I might have had, I decided to focus primarily on the star that was associated with each Watcher. By doing this I was able to rule out my preconceived ideas. This proved to be very effective for me, and the results were a bit surprising, as you will see. The rituals were performed in the woods outside of my home town and were continued for about five months. Results came faster than I had expected, but I did have several failures in the process. The ritual was a simple calling of the Watcher to appear, and I burned Solomon's seal root as a base for the Watcher to appear in.

Watcher of the North

The night air was very cold as I prepared the circle and waited for the Watcher of the North. This Watcher is associated with the star

Fomalhaut, so that was the first thing that I looked for. The night sky was somewhat cloudy, but I had enough open sky to locate the star and begin the ceremony. The moon was just entering into its waning phase, but the scattered clouds offered some shading from the brightness of the moon, thus allowing me to see the stars a little clearer.

I began the ceremony at about 10:25, with the results coming, I would imagine, at about 11:00. At first I thought perhaps the ritual was not working properly, but then I saw some movement in the shadows of the northern quarter and in the distance, I could hear dogs howling. A chill swept over my body, and I knew that something was coming. Still repeating the long request for the Watcher to appear, I placed a handful of the Solomon's seal root onto the burning coals and closed my eyes, awaiting the approach of the Northern Watcher.

I felt a "shift" in my conscious mind, and when I opened my eyes I saw before me a magnificent translucent being. I was taken aback by the black robe, as I had expected green to be the dominant color of this Watcher, due to its association with the North and with the element Earth. Also, my impression of the Watchers has always been that they are masculine, but this being was markedly female in nature.

She must have picked up my thoughts, as spirits do, because at that point she spoke. "Not at all what you thought I would be?" she asked. Her voice is hard to describe, but I would describe it as feminine with very deep tones. I asked for the sign that she was indeed the Watcher of the North and she smiled.

Satisfied that I had the being that I was hoping to contact, I began the process of communing with the Watcher. I asked as to what role she played in the craft, to which she answered that, overall, her purpose was the same as the others, and that was to watch over the rites and protect the circle from any unwanted spirits or energies. Also, the Watchers act as guides in the afterlife. Over the years, the craft was suppressed and the Watchers were called upon for a different task, that being to search out potential witches and bring them into the craft by guiding new people to the proper locations so that they may learn the ways. The conversation continued on a personal level, as there were things that I wished to know about my personal life as well as some of my past lives. I was assured that this was not the first time I had contacted this Watcher. Then I gave thanks to this Watcher and pledged my friendship.

With this, she retreated into the shadows of the trees, and I was overcome with a deep sense of strength, that I could accomplish anything. If I had at anytime in my life a need to be consoled or counseled, this would be the Watcher that I would come to. Guidance was the key word that came into my mind, and I was nearly overwhelmed by this Watcher's personality. Supporting and offering strength in times of great need are the primary attributes of the Watcher of the North.

Watcher of the East

I was very excited to work with the Eastern Watcher, as the star that is associated with him is Aldeboran, located in the constellation of Taurus. This star has always called to me for some reason, and it was the first star that I ever identified in the night sky.

To locate it, simply find the constellation of Orion. When you have located Orion's belt, follow an imaginary line to the right, along the angle of Orion's belt and there you will find Aldeboran. It is a bright star that shines with a noticeably red color.

Having located it, I cast the circle and began the ritual to call the Watcher in. I felt the presence of the Eastern Watcher much sooner than the Northern Watcher and would guess that he appeared in only about 15 minutes. A slow and steady breeze preceded his appearance, and when I opened my eyes I saw before me the Watcher of the East.

A masculine form, thin and very luminescent, wearing a long, sheer, white robe.

Once again, this totally threw me off, as I had expected yellow, orange, or even red, as Aldeboran is a red star and often associated with the planet Mars. Although masculine in form, this Watcher had features that were somewhat feminine. His face was very thin and beautiful, and in his hand he carried a small vial of scented oil. The overall view of him was stunning and brilliant, with a soft and controlled voice.

When I was certain that this was the Watcher of the East, I began my questions. The Eastern Watcher's nature is that of a mediator. He gives advice and helps to find balance when and where it is needed. Much of the information that I needed about these beings was given to me by the Northern Watcher. I really wanted to get an idea of what the "feel" of each Watcher was. With the Eastern Watcher I felt a sense of justice and authority. The energy was not as caring as the Northern Watcher, but still there was a feeling of comfort and protection. When I had completed my questions and gave thanks, the Watcher disappeared and all that remained was the smoke of the Solomon's seal and the still night air.

Watcher of the South

The Southern Watcher is associated with the star Regulus, located in the constellation Leo. The presence of this Watcher was almost overwhelming to me. He appeared to me in a vibrant red robe and about his head, going around like the petals of a flower, were small dancing rays of orangish-red light. This image fit in with what my mind had expected.

He informed me that his duties are that of a judge and dispenser of penalties. For this reason he does not often get involved with individuals on a personal level, making our conversation straight and to the point. He is associated with karmic retribution and is invoked to help with passing judgments or making decisions of great importance. This Watcher was straightforward and did not stay for any personal questions. Once the information was given, he bid me farewell and vanished.

Watcher of the West

This Watcher is associated with the star Antares, which is located in the constellation Scorpio. This ritual was difficult for me, as it occurred at a time of the year when the only time that Antares is visible is at 5:45 a.m. The star appeared just above the trees at near daybreak, making the peacefulness of the night limited in time. After several failed attempts, I finally succeeded.

This Watcher appeared to me, and once again I was surprised as a beautiful feminine figure stood before me with flowing gray robes that were constantly in motion. In her hand she held a large snake of a type that I could not identify.

Our visit was brief, and she told me that her duties were to be the giver of emotion and unconditional love. She is invoked to bring emotional balance as well as to help stir the emotions of a person who is cold or frigid. The feel of this Watcher is one of absolute affection. I felt as though I could have remained in her presence for the rest of my life and never once been unhappy. I do believe that this is the danger of this Watcher as well as the blessing of it. As the daylight began to show she bid me farewell and disappeared, leaving only the smoke of the incense.

The most important thing that I learned from working with these Watchers is that they are not representations of the four elements, but are stellar spirits who are associated with the directions of the quarters.

In working closely with these Watchers, I was able to get a better grasp as to why they are to be invoked during rituals. Do not forget them when you cast your circles and do not fear them. They are there to help us and protect us, not as our slaves or servants, but as our friends and companions. They help to guide our lives and our ways.

CHAPTER 12

INVOCATION: SUMMONING SPIRITS AND DEITIES

Then said Saul unto his servants, Seek me a woman that hath a familiar spirit, that I may go to her and enquire of her.

I SAMUEL 28.7, *THE HOLY BIBLE*

A familiar is a spirit or animal that becomes a companion and aid to the witch in his or her magical practices. The word *familiar* comes from the Latin word *famulus*, meaning an attendant. Another word that some witches use is magistellus, which means "little master."

A familiar should not be confused with the Native American concept of the totem animal. The totem animal is the essence or spiritual force that resides in certain animals that can be tapped into through shamanic practices to bring about a change in the shaman's or witch's personality. The totem is used to effect change in the self more than in the outer world. While the two practices are similar, there are various differences. Totems are called upon mostly when a person needs a certain quality that that animal is associated with. For example, if I have a need to be clever and stealthy, I can call upon the fox totem.

A familiar I would use to simply go out and do the work I need done. For example, if I am going for a job interview, I can send my familiar spirit out to see that my application gets looked at before any others. This may seem a bit far-fetched, but the familiar spirit is very effective. A familiar can be used for divination, spell casting, healing, or any purpose the witch desires.

While there are those who practice the craft today who feel that magick should be an expression of personal power generated by the witch and that working with spirits is not part of traditional witch-craft, I can only say that as an individual there is only so much that one witch can do. Spirits offer a way to help others in ways that one person could not. Also, a witch does not command or demand that a spirit serve as a slave. The witch befriends the spirit, and favors are asked in return for favors granted, just as you might ask a friend to help with a problem. There have been times when I did not ask a familiar spirit to help, but the spirit did so out of kindness and friend-ship anyway. As long as you do not fall into the trap of believing that you are the all-powerful controller of the spirit realm, you have little or nothing to fear from working with spirits.

A familiar can come in one of three forms: a discarnate spirit of a deceased human, a nonhuman entity such as an elemental spirit, or an actual animal.

A RITE TO SUMMON AN ELEMENTAL SPIRIT FAMILIAR

In the realms of spirit, there live a certain species of spirits which are the embodiment of the energies of the primal elements of Earth, Air, Fire and Water.

—*JOURNAL OF LORD CORVUS OF THESSALY (1989)*

Preliminary Work

You should, prior to this ritual, bathe in an infusion that is associated with the particular element you wish to engage. For example, if you wish to work with a fire elemental, bathe in a fire bath; for a gnome, an earth bath (see chapter 7 for recipes).

Once you have decided which type of elemental spirit you wish to work with, you should prepare an object to house that spirit. To do this you should go on a quest to search for the object. In olden days, a rounded red stone was the most sought-after object. Remember, this object cannot be purchased, but must be found. Beaches, parks, stone quarries, railways, or woods are the best places to look for these objects. The quest should be done on a Tuesday, and you should begin as early in the morning as possible.

When you wake up, bathe and anoint yourself on the third eye, hands, and bottom of the feet with attraction oil or olive oil while you say the following:

At this early hour, on this Tuesday,
Do I set out on my way.
I seek for that which I desire
In patch of wood, roadside, or briar.
A stone, a bottle, a stick or feather
To house my familiar spirit together.
A comfortable home for my familiar I look;
I search through every cranny and nook.
Guide me to the object most right
So that I can meet my familiar tonight.

Wander about for a while and search for the object. Eventually, you will find it. There will be something that catches your eye. Do not rush this, but just allow it to happen. Be patient and keep a sharp eye.

Remember that the object should be small enough to keep in your pocket or perhaps be fashioned into some jewelry.

Once you have the object, thank the spirit or deity that has guided you to it and take it home with you to begin preparing it. First, you should infuse the object with the same element as that of the spirit. So if you are going to house an Air spirit, blow repeatedly on the object or, if it is a windy day, hold it out in the wind. If it is a Fire spirit, then pass it three times through the flame of a candle; if a Water spirit, then soak it in pure spring water; and if an Earth spirit, bury it in some soil for a while. This step can be substituted with the soaking of the object in the appropriate elemental bath.

Once the object is infused with the power of the element, then you are ready to begin the summoning of the elemental spirit into the object. Note that the difference between this way of summoning and that associated with ceremonial magick, is that the witch does not command the spirit to enter the object and bind it there, but rather asks the spirit if it would be willing to remain in the object as a magical companion. A witch desires to live in harmony with all beings, both of this world and all other worlds. Thus a ceremonial magician will have a serving spirit and a witch will have a familiar spirit.

ITEMS NEEDED:

- The object the spirit will occupy (Spiritus Loci)
- Powdered eggshell
- Solomon's seal root (cut)
- Self-lighting charcoal
- 3 green seven-day candles (for life)
- A sharp needle
- Incense appropriate to the element of the spirit you have chosen

The Spell

This ritual is designed to summon the elemental spirit into the object that you have chosen to house it. Arrange your altar with the three green candles forming a downward pointing triangle. Place the Spiritus Loci directly in the center of these three candles. Place all other objects off to the side. Begin by casting your ritual circle, but do not summon the elemental powers. Call the Watchers to witness and protect and then begin the process of invocation.

Turn and face the direction of the element that you have chosen. Earth in the north, Air in the east, Fire in the south, and Water in the west. Face the direction and say:

Mighty Spirits of the Element Earth (Air, Fire, Water), *I do summon you to attend this Rite and grant thy aid and power unto my task. I beseech thee to come to my aid on this day* (night), *and one of you to enter this* (name the object) *and work with me as my magical companion. I give this offering of incense to you.*

Place some of the elemental incense on the charcoal and then place a pinch of Solomon's seal on top of that. Sit before your altar and stare at the object. The incense burner should be placed so that it is between the object and your line of view.

At this point, you should gaze into the rising smoke. Discern the patterns that the smoke makes as it rises upward. Within the smoke you will see the shape of the spirit that will become your familiar. This shape can and will vary from witch to witch, so do not feel as though you did not see the correct figure. When you see the spirit appear in the rising smoke, take up the object and hold it above the burning incense so that the smoke touches it. Once this is done, place the object back in the center of the candles and sprinkle the object with powdered egg shell to help "feed" it. If you do not see the spirit within the smoke right away, place more incense and Solomon's seal onto the charcoal and continue gazing into the smoke and repeating the call until you do.

Once the spirit has entered the object, say the following:

> *Thank you O' Spirit Familiar for coming to aid me in my time*
> *of need.*
> *Let us be as one in both mind and in deed.*
> *To work powerful magick for the good of any and all and*
> *show that a witch's power does indeed enthrall.*
> *I pray thee do not abandon me neither night nor day;*
> *But within this* (object) *do stay.*
> *That when I have a need of thee or thee of me,*
> *That close together we shall be.*

Allow the object to remain in the center of the triangle of candles until they have burned out. The energy of these candles will help "feed" the familiar spirit and allow it to grow in strength. Once the candles have extinguished, you must feed your familiar spirit from time to time. It is best to do this everyday, but it can be done once a week. Either way, it is important that you try to communicate continually with the spirit. If you do not, then the link between the two of you will never fully connect, and the spirit will eventually leave.

Uses for the Elemental Spirit

What do you do with the familiar spirit? How can it help in your magical practices? The familiar spirit can be used instead of having to cast a spell for every little thing. The familiar spirit can be sent to perform the task at hand. This is done by first feeding the spirit and then by requesting the service of the spirit. Tell it what you would like to accomplish and be as specific as possible. In the example below I give the technique that I used to secure a certain job that I wanted.

After putting in my application at the place I wished to work, I went before my familiar spirit's home and placed an offering of wine. In my mind I recalled the image of my familiar as it appeared to me in the smoke during the previous ritual. Then I saw it step out of the object, take a sip of wine and ask me what my request was. I asked that it go to the place where my application was and make certain that the person in charge of hiring saw my application. "Place my application on top of the stack and make sure that it gets seen."

With this done, the familiar vanished and I went about my usual daily routine. The next morning, I received a phone call from the company I wished to work for. They had reviewed my application and were very pleased with what they had seen. Now this might have seemed like a normal incident had the personnel director not told me what happened next.

He said that it seemed as though I was supposed to be hired because he had reviewed my application first and put it aside. He then began going through the rest of the stack and came across my application again a little further down. At first he thought that perhaps I had put in two applications, but when he looked through the pile that he had previous looked at, mine was not there. He thought perhaps that he had unknowingly put it back in the stack he was viewing. Then he said that when he had finished going through the applications he was placing them back into his file cabinet when my application slipped out of his hand and fell to the floor. If that were not enough, when he returned to work the following morning, my application was sitting on his desk.

Now, this may seem an amazing story, but it is the truth and is a perfect example of what a witch can do with the help of a familiar. With this in mind comes the question, "If a familiar can do that, why can't it go and manipulate the lottery or other games of chance and make one a millionaire?" The answer is, "It can."

But remember that as a witch you must live in accordance with the laws of the universe. A witch does not seek to break these laws, only to bend them. To ask to win the lottery jackpot and be extremely wealthy might cause more problems than it is worth. An example of this is what happened to Alex Sanders when he used his magick to solve all of his financial problems. He was soon adopted by a very wealthy couple who felt that he reminded them of their dead son. All of his finances were taken care of, and he no longer had to worry about money. But hardship came in other forms, and his life was no better off than it was before he was financially secure. A comfortable life is all that the witch desires, not necessarily an easy one.

RITE TO SUMMON A DISCARNATE SPIRIT FAMILIAR

Forthwith the wolves take to flights, their talons loosened, the birds fly unfed, while the Thessalian witch selects her prophet......and in the dead body seeks a voice.

—LUCAN, *PHARSALIA*

There are very few people I know who would perform this particular spell, but for those of you with strong hearts and a love for the morbid and the Underworld deities, this ritual will not leave you disappointed.

Preliminary work

Prior to this ritual, you should bath in a spiritual bath consisting of Solomon's seal root and wormwood.

ITEMS NEEDED

- Parchment paper or regular typing paper
- 1 egg
- Piece of raw meat
- Bowl of graveyard dust (from within a tomb, not the ground)
- Your athame
- Ambrosia

The Spell

Cast your ritual circle in the usual manner. Face the western quarter and say:

> *Behold ye gods and goddesses of the Western Land of the Dead. I stand here before you anointed and cleansed as is proper. Watch over and protect me from all things profane and grant me that which I desire. Communication with those who dwell within your realm. Guide me to the one who can answer my request.*

At this point, raise your hands high and say:

> *The dead shall rise and come to me.*

At this point, open a portal to your circle and go to the closest graveyard. This should be done at night. Before entering the grave-yard, you must pour a libation of ambrosia for the deities who rule the Underworld. Only in this way will they allow the spirits of the dead to leave their domain for a short time to help you.

Begin to wander the cemetery. Allow yourself to be drawn to a certain spot. This will not be difficult, as the gods are now directing your movements. The spell works best if you can find the grave of the most recently buried person. However, if you are led to an older grave, work with that one. The trick is that this spell only works with the spirits of people who have not yet reincarnated. When you find a grave that you feel is the one you need, you kneel before it and read the name aloud. Thus will you fix the name in your memory, as you will need it later. Write the name three times reversed on parchment (which is more traditional, but regular paper will do) and say the following:

> *By the powers of witchcraft do I summon forth the spirits of the dead.* (Name), *leave your somber place of habitation and cross the River Styx back into the land of the living. By the powers of the gods and goddesses of the Underworld, do I summon you back that you may appear to me in the hour I choose.*

Take the graveyard dust and sprinkle it to the four directions, saying:

> *May* (name of deceased), *who is dust return from the dust, awake from your sleep and answer unto my call and my demand. This do I ask in the names of the gods and goddesses of the Underworld and with their permission.*

Place the egg upon the grave, rise, turn, and leave the graveyard. As you exit, toss the piece of raw meat over your shoulder without looking back. This is to appease any negative spirits that may try to follow you. They will drain the life force within the raw meat and leave you on your way.

Return to your circle and place the parchment with the name beneath your skrying mirror or bowl. Light a charcoal and burn some incense compounded of sandalwood and lavender while you chant the name of the person three times. There should be only two candles lit on either side of the mirror or bowl so that their light illuminates the surface but does not reflect the candle. Gaze steadily into the mirror or water, and in a short time, the face of the person whose name is beneath it should appear within the surface of the skrying tool and be able to converse with you.

Ask the questions you wish to have answered or give the spirit instructions for what you want done. Keep in mind the tenet of Perfect Love and Perfect Trust and do not ask spirits or entities to do harmful things to others. When all is done, you must take the parchment with the name on it and set it on fire. Be careful that you catch all of the ashes and keep them safe. On the following night, return to the grave of the person you have summoned. Be certain to leave an offering of ambrosia again. Scatter the ashes onto the tomb or ground around the grave saying:

> *From ashes have I brought* (name) *forth*
> *To ashes now I send thee back.*
> *With thanks for the work thou hast done,*
> *Many blessing of the gods upon you.*

If the egg that you placed on your first visit is still there, take it up and crack it. If it is not there, rest assured that whoever found it has thrown it out and is wondering what it was there for. It is not necessary to throw another piece of meat for the negative spirits, but if you wish to do so, it surely would not hurt.

When you have returned from your final visit to the graveyard, it is of the utmost importance that you fumigate yourself and the room in which the ritual was held with sulfur. Do not inhale the fumes, as they can be quite nauseating, but fumigate the entire room and yourself. This should be done anytime that you come in contact with the dead. Sulfur repels all energies associated with otherworld spirits and entities. If this is not done, you run the risk of exposing yourself to the actions of malicious spirits or spirits of the dead congregating in your ritual room and creating a somber and sorrowful feeling to all who enter.

Once your chamber is cleansed, you should take a spiritual cleansing bath consisting of rue, rosemary, and lavender. This removes negative vibrations and opens the aura to receive positive vibrations.

Another important note to this ritual is that you must not keep the spirit of this deceased person as your permanent familiar, even if you are requested to do so. To do this would inhibit their spiritual progression and prevent their own attainment of goals and accomplishments in future lives. This could result in great catastrophe for you and the deceased.

SUMMONING AN ANIMAL SPIRIT FAMILIAR

Another way in which the animal familiar was used was to convey a magical influence, for good or evil, to another person.

—DOREEN VALIENTE, *THE ABC OF WITCHCRAFT*

I cannot count the number of times I have been asked how to summon an animal familiar, or how an animal becomes a witch's familiar. The process is the same as summoning an elemental spirit familiar, with one exception. Instead of requesting to find an object to house your familiar spirit, you ask to find an animal to be your familiar spirit. This is the only difference. If you already have an animal that you would like to become your familiar spirit, then you should request for the spirit to work through that animal. This is not harmful to the animal in any way, shape, or form.

The animal that becomes the vessel for a familiar spirit will often display very human qualities. I once had a cat named Milo who was my familiar. Milo displayed features so human that many of my friends were frightened by him. He was, first off, an enormous animal, and his fur was a beautiful blue-gray that shined like velvet. Milo would not eat from the floor, not even from a bowl on the floor. His bowl needed to be placed on the table across from where I was eating. To top that quirk, Milo would not lower his face into his bowl to eat, but lifted his food to his mouth using his paws! When you looked to him and talked, he responded with a series of "meows" that were almost intelligible. I could go on and on about Milo, but I think instead I should tell you how to go about working with an animal familiar.

To request a service of your animal familiar is simple. You pick the animal up, hold it, pet it, and state your request. Now, the animal is not going to go to the window and fly off to do your task. Instead, when the animal is asleep, the spirit that operates through it will leave to go and do your task.

This is why cats are a good choice for familiars. Cats sleep most of the time and therefore are faster workers. In ancient times, however, pigs were the most common familiars. This was mostly because owning a cat could be used as evidence against you should it be discovered that you were a witch. Also, it is important to understand that when you choose an animal for a familiar, you cannot just get rid of it one day because it has grown old and is no longer cute and fluffy. Once a spirit has taken residence in the animal, that spirit and that animal are your responsibility until the animal dies or the spirit decides to leave.

In Milo's case, I awoke one morning and he was gone. It was one of the most heart-wrenching experiences I have ever gone through, and till this day I have never had another animal familiar; I much prefer the permanent companionship of an elemental spirit familiar.

THE GREAT RITE

One of the most sacred and controversial rites of witchcraft is known as the Great Rite. In ancient times, it was called the *Hieros Gamos*, or Divine Marriage, and was an invocational rite where a priest and priestess invoke a god and goddess into themselves and then engage in sexual union. Through this sacred union, the fertility of the city or worshippers was guaranteed.

In modern witchcraft, there are not many people who follow the actual Great Rite, but for those of you who wish to perform this sacred act, then here is the outline for it. Remember always that no one should be coerced or forced into performing this rite. Both parties must be willing. To actually perform this rite in full, you would need someone well versed in the process of invocations to call the deities down into the priest and priestess. Otherwise, you would only invite the deities into the circle and have them draw the energy of the sexual union to strengthen their presence and connection with the priest and priestess.

Performance of The Great Rite

The circle is cast in the usual manner, and all lights should be extinguished except for the quarter candles and the altar candles. The priest should begin the invocation of the goddess into the priestess by holding the wand above the head of the priestess saying:

> *Thee, O great Goddess, do I call upon to descend into this thy Priestess that we may be joined in union and partake of the Sacred Elixirs of Life and Light. By leaf and flower, by root and stem, by seed and fruit do I call upon thee to descend into the body of this Priestess and be with us here this night.*

This is repeated over and over again until the presence of the goddess descends into the priestess. When this is done, if the priestess is not taken fully, she may in turn invoke the god into the priest. If the priestess is taken fully, then it will be the maiden's responsibility to invoke the god into the priest. This is done by holding the wand above the priest's head and saying the following:

O Great God, as height calls on deep, so does your Goddess call on thee. In her name do I call upon thee to descend into this thy Priest that you may share in the pleasures of union. For we know that you delight in the beauty of woman, and so by leaf and flower, by root and stem, by seed and fruit do I call upon thee to descend into the body of this Priest and be with us here this night.

This is repeated over and over again until the god descends into the body of the priest. At this point, things can get a little tricky. Ideally, both priest and priestess should be completely taken by the god and goddess and from there on would engage in sexual intercourse. The rest of the coven would either leave the circle or remain within with their backs turned. I believe that remaining in the circle is the best option, as the coven gets to experience the intense energy that is generated by this act. It also brings a unification of energy and brings the coven closer together as a family.

If the Priest and/or Priestess is not taken fully by the deities, then a ritual play must be acted out. This play goes as follows:

PRIEST: *Now I must reveal a great mystery.*

The priestess lies down, face upward, in the center of the circle with her head pointing north and feet pointing south. This aligns the priestess with the natural flow of magnetic (i.e., goddess) energy of the Earth.

The Priest then kneels beside her, facing west, and begins the following speech. The symbol * signifies that the priest kisses the priestess just above the pubic area, except in the two instances where it is otherwise noted.)

I. PRIEST: *Assist me to erect the ancient altar, at which in days past all worshipped,*
    The Great Altar of all things;

For in olden times, Woman was the altar.
Thus was the altar made and placed;
And the sacred point was the point within the center of the circle.
As we have of old been taught that the point within the center is the source of all things.
Therefore should we adore it. (*)
Therefore whom we adore we also invoke, by the power of the Lifted Lance.
(At the word "lance" the priest touches his own penis.)
O' Circle of Stars (*)
Whereof our father is but the younger brother (*)
Marvel beyond imagination, soul of infinite space,
Before whom time is bewildered and understanding dark,
Not unto thee may we attain unless thine image be love. (*)
Therefore by seed and root, by stem and bud, by leaf and flower and fruit,
Do we invoke thee,
O Queen of Space, O dew of light,
Continuous One of the heavens (*)
Let it be ever thus, that men speak not of thee as one, but as none;
And let them not speak of thee at all, since thou art continuous.
For thou art the point within the circle (*) which we adore (*),
The fount of life without which we would not be (*)
And in this way are erected the Twin Pillars (kisses the left breast, the right breast).
In beauty and in strength were they erected,
To the wonder and glory of all men.

II. At this point, all coveners, except the priest and priestess, either turn their backs or leave the ritual circle. When all is still and silent, the priest continues:

PRIEST: *O Secret of Secrets,*
That art hidden in the being of all lives,
Not thee do we adore,
For that which adoreth is also thou.
Thou art That, and That am I. (*)
I am the flame that burns in the heart of every man,
And in the core of every star.
I am life, and the giver of life.
Yet therefore is the knowledge of me the knowledge of death.
I am alone, the Lord within ourselves,
Whose name is Mystery of Mysteries.

III. Now the priest kisses the priestess in the following manner: above the pubic area, on the right foot, the left knee, the right knee, left foot, and above the pubic area. [This forms a pentagram.] Now the priest kisses the lips, left breast, right breast, and then the lips again. [This forms a triangle.] The two combined, i.e., the triangle above the pentagram, is the symbol for a third degree witch. Now the Priest gently lays his body over the body of the priestess and says:

PRIEST: *Make open the path of intelligence between us,*
For these truly are the Five points of Fellowship—
Foot to foot,
Knee to knee,
Lance to Grail,
Breast to Breast,
Lips to lips. (kisses priestess on lips)

By the Great and holy name (name of god that is invoked),
in the name of (name of goddess invoked),
Encourage our hearts;
Let the light crystallize itself in our blood,
Fulfilling of us resurrection.
For there is no part of us that is not of the Gods.

The rite is concluded by ritual lovemaking. This should be a sharing of souls between priest and priestess and not thought of as an act of mere physical pleasure. This rite, when done with the correct frame of mind and attitude, is the most beautiful and moving rite I have ever seen or performed.

In part I of the rite we have the priest adoring the priestess and the embodiment of womanhood. The vagina of the priestess is directly in the center of the circle, and it is this "point within the center of the circle" that the priest makes reference to as the source of all things.

This is absolute reverence for the birth-giving properties of the woman. Each of us, whether man or woman, are here as a direct result of birth, and thus the vagina is the source of all things. It is the symbol of life; "thus should we adore it."

A sentence that causes some confusion to people reading or hearing this rite is the line that reads, "of which our Father is but the younger brother." This is a reference to the myths of the goddess and god in relation to the Sabbats and/or seasons of the year. The goddess falls in love with the Sun god, only to have him die and descend into the realms of death. The goddess then seeks him out in the Underworld only to find that he is now transformed into the god of Death. In her absence and in the absence of the Sun god, the world grows cold, and winter sets upon the Middle World. As Death, the god asks for her hand, but she refuses to accept his love, for he, Death, causes all that she loves to wither and die. Death explains that it is time and age that cause things to die, not him, and once this is understood, the goddess receives his hand and they join together. She conceives a son for the god of Death, and gives birth to the Sun god, whom she sends to the Middle World to bring warmth back to the land. The goddess then longs for the Middle World that she has left, and in secret she leaves the dark lord behind and returns. She then sees the Sun god and falls in love, and the cycle continues. Thus are both the god of Death and the god of the Sun brothers as well as father and son. If this seems confusing, you are quite right. To fully understand this myth cycle, you must experience it through the seasons.

The twin pillars referred to in part I of the Great Rite are, of course, referring to the breasts of the priestess. Nearly all ancient temples had two great pillars or columns that marked the entryway into the inner chamber of worship. Thus are the breasts the pillars of Beauty and Strength, which lead down to the sacred point within the circle.

In part II of the Great Rite the priest, after having adored and revered the goddess in part I, now reveals his role in the act of creation. In this part the priest identifies himself with the powers of manhood and reveals to the priestess his mysteries. Even though he is Life and the power of Life, to know him is to know Death. For remember the mystery of the myth, the god of Life (the Sun) is also the god of Death and vice versa. One cannot know Life without eventually knowing Death, so the two are interdependent and part of the same process. Thus is the god known as the Mystery of Mysteries.

Part III of the Great Rite is the actual union of the god and goddess. The priest lying on top of the priestess and requesting that the pathway of intelligence be opened between them is the statement of fact that when two people join in sexual union, it is not simply a biological function but a sharing of energies, and it opens lines of communication that connect them psychically to each other, joined in the true way of fellowship, with bodies embraced together. Then, of course, comes the powerful statement, "there is no part of us that is not of the gods." This I think is the most moving part of the rite. This statement says it all. We are all divine, and each of us is an aspiring god or goddess and thus deserve to be treated with respect and honor. So mote it be!

The Symbolic Great Rite

Today, most covens do not perform the Great Rite in actuality, but opt to perform it symbolically. This is done, for the most part, during the rite called "Cakes and Ale." The symbolic Great Rite is very short and simple and goes as follows.

The priest kneels before the priestess holding the chalice of wine or ale up to her. She takes her athame and lowers the tip of the athame into the wine and says:

> *As Athame is to male, so is the Chalice to female.*
> *The Union of both, is the blessing of all.*

This is a simple rite that substitutes the sexual union of man and woman with the symbolism of the athame (male phallus) and the chalice (female vagina). This rite does not pack anywhere near the psychic energy of the actual Great Rite, but it does work and can be used in ritual.

Appendix

COLORS AND THEIR MAGICAL PROPERTIES

White - purification, peace, protection, and spiritual purification

Black - cursing, removing negativity (by absorption), sadness, loss, and confusion

Green - money, prosperity, fertility, and luck

Brown - fast money, hesitation, robs energy, and neutralizing

Yellow - stimulates intellect, divination, increases memory, brings visions

Orange - controlling a person or situation, protection in legal matters, and success

Red - promotes lust, sexual desire, passion, and gives energy

Blue - peace in the home, healing, and induces sleep

Gold - helps in finding jobs, prosperity, good luck

Grey - neutralizes negative energy, cancels the effects of gossip, and halts psychic or magical attacks

Purple - conquering, overcoming obstacles, healing serious illnesses

Pink - love, friendships, and fidelity